advanced
bread baking
at Home

advanced
bread baking
at Home

Recipes & Techniques
to Perfect Your
Sourdough and More

chef daniele brenci
Creator of Breadcrumb

PAGE STREET
PUBLISHING CO.

PAGE STREET
PUBLISHING CO.

First published in 2021 by
Page Street Publishing Co.
27 Congress Street, Suite 105
Salem, MA 01970
www.pagestreetpublishing.com

Distributed by Macmillan, sales in Canada by The Canadian Manda Group.

25   24   23   22   21   1   2   3   4   5

ISBN-13: 978-1-64567-460-3
ISBN-10: 1-64567-460-6

Library of Congress Control Number: 2021931383

Cover and book design by Laura Benton for Page Street Publishing Co.
Photography by Daniele Brenci

Printed and bound in the United States

Page Street Publishing protects our planet by donating to nonprofits like The Trustees, which focuses on local land conservation.

This book was written during the COVID-19 pandemic, and it is dedicated to all of the people who have found a positive outlet in baking during the challenging times that we have all faced across the globe. I am hoping you will take what you have learned during this time we have been forced to spend apart and share it with those you love most now that you are reunited.

Contents

introduction

Grains were one of the first ever consumed foods. As society evolved, bread quickly became a staple food that, to this day, represents the very foundation of nutritional needs as well as being an essential component of many culinary traditions. Bread in its many forms is often the vessel different cultures use to deliver their flavors. For example, in Rome when grandma asks you to try her tomato sauce that's been simmering on the stove all day, you sure don't grab a spoon, but rather you tear off a piece of bread and dip that in the pot. You would never waste an opportunity like that with a spoon! Similarly, flatbreads are used in cuisines around the world to accompany and wrap some of the most flavorful foods. I could never imagine an Indian feast without naan bread or Middle Eastern food without pita. From Southeast Asia to Central and South America, traveling through the Middle East, Africa and Europe, countless varieties of bread exist. Grains have transformed over time, evolving into some of the most delicious creations.

In this book I aim to refresh and refine your baking skills. If you're just beginning to explore the craft, I'd like to guide you through the process starting from scratch, beginning with the very basics of how I go about the process of baking, from sourcing quality ingredients to choosing the right equipment and developing and maintaining your own sourdough culture. Once you have progressed through the initial steps successfully, the real fun begins. I am excited to share with you my exploration of some more advanced techniques. I start with a tribute to ancient grains and classic breads, where the mastery of sourdough baking combined with the knowledge of the performance of each individual grain will allow you to develop a successful loaf that highlights the flavor, texture and unique qualities of these distinct grains. Moving forward through the book, I explore more playful applications of flavor combinations and techniques that I hope will encourage you to experiment on your own and will stimulate your creativity.

You will soon learn how deep my love for pizza is, which is why I wanted to dedicate a whole chapter to pizza and focaccia. Historically, pizza has taken many shapes over time in different regions of Italy and around the world. In fact, I thought the pizza I grew up eating in Rome was the only way pizza was supposed to be made, and I was under the impression that there were only two main styles, Roman and Neapolitan. Once I landed in the United States years ago, I found out how this profoundly celebrated and avidly protected Italian masterpiece was transformed into so many exquisite variations. Often taking the name of the cities in which they were mastered, a new pizza world opened up in front of me. It was fascinating to see how a few inches of dough topped with a handful of simple ingredients have so powerfully brought people and cultures closer together to celebrate what ultimately is something we all enjoy sharing: bread.

Celebrating with food is a profound tradition deep within my roots. I believe that the gesture of tearing bread with your hands and sharing it over a warm meal with others is one of the purest forms of spreading love and joy, which is why I feel particularly attached to baking. Bread is meant to be enjoyed with others, so I wrote this book to share what I've learned over the years cooking and baking. My goal is to help you on your journey, whether you have never baked before or you're a professional looking for inspiration. Within the pages of this book, I have aimed to embrace both my heritage and traditions as well as playfulness and innovation from my experience as a professionally trained chef, and I am excited to take you along on my baking journey.

how i got here

My younger brother and I were raised by a single mom, the most beautiful, hard-working woman who showed us nothing but love and support. She worked four jobs to keep things in order at home. To help out, I would make lunch for my brother and myself. These were my earliest attempts at making food. My mother didn't have much time to spend in the kitchen, but despite her long days she always managed to fix us something delicious in the evening.

When school was on break, we would spend a lot of time at my grandma's. She and my grandfather inherited some land in a small town just outside of Rome where they built their home and over the years grew their own micro farm. My grandma's garden was majestic, and still is to this day. The house is surrounded by fruit trees, strawberries and spontaneous herbs and flowers. Figs, apricots, peaches, grapes, cherries and hazelnuts are just a few of the flavors I grew up enjoying right off the trees.

I remember after summer helping my grandma pick olives from her trees to get them ready for extraction. The satisfaction of starting the day with fresh olives and ending it with the most fragrant and intense olive oil drizzled on a warm bruschetta is something I will never forget. We would spend countless hours foraging the forest around her property learning how to make use of every single ingredient. My grandma's passion for nature and food has defined the very foundation of how I perceive food and ultimately inspired me to become the curious chef I am today.

I grew up in Rome, a place closely attached to its history and customs. I deeply love everything the city has to offer me, from the people to the lifestyle and traditions, but most of all the amazing food. I will never forget nights out with friends. We would always meet at some local trattoria where the most beautiful spreads of food were laid out on intimate small tables. Specialties like carbonara, amatriciana, cacio e pepe, local cheese and salumi, just to name a few, were must-haves. They were always served alongside some fresh baked bread and house wine, and dinner's grand finale was gelato and pastries. Basically, all we do in Italy is eat! If you aren't eating, you're probably thinking about what your next meal is going to be.

I remember sneaking into the local bakery early in the morning before getting home after a long night out where my friends and I would consume enormous quantities of croissants just out of the oven. I was always the last one among my friends to leave. I would find myself asking the bakers clothed in all white and covered in flour from head to toe if they could show me what they were making. I would follow them closely across the slippery floor to peek at some of the preparations and ask tons of questions until they finally had enough of me and kicked me out.

The baking world intrigued me so much. The focaccia and croissants are just a different experience to bite into when they are still warm fresh out of the oven. It was mesmerizing to see the long wooden peels pulling out dozens of warm loaves of bread and ciabatta from those infinitely deep ovens. I could not believe the amount of bread they were baking in those ovens all at once.

I started culinary school out of curiosity. I loved food but wasn't particularly attracted to cooking, nor was I aware of the strict and rigorous culture of professional kitchens. While finishing my years of school I started working dinner shifts at a traditional restaurant in the center of the city. I did love baking but couldn't pursue the craft while in school because bakers worked night shifts and I had to be in class in the morning. I had no idea what to expect from working in a restaurant. Food was handled in such an artistic way; it was vibrant, with so many different elements and techniques I had never seen before. Not to mention the rush of dinner service. I was hooked.

Soon after graduating from culinary school I decided to leave my beloved Rome. My best friend had just moved to London a few months prior, and so I decided to join him in what turned out to be an amazing journey. We didn't speak a word of English and had barely any money saved. We rented a room together and I started looking for work. I would show up to Michelin-starred restaurants trying to speak with the chef, asking for a job in my very poor broken English. I was rejected many times until I was finally hired at a French restaurant. I was ecstatic for the opportunity to prove myself.

It was just months later that I moved to a different restaurant where I ultimately met the head chef who brought me to the United States for a restaurant opening. He told me about the opportunity, and we flew to Malibu the very next day. I was promoted to sous chef and was joined by part of the team from London. We opened this massive restaurant just a few feet from the water. It was beautiful.

Since moving to the States, I have transitioned from the fast pace of the Michelin-starred restaurant world to working as a private chef while traveling from Malibu to Chicago and most recently to Pittsburgh. The choice of working as a private chef has allowed me to dedicate more time to my creativity, and a few years ago I finally started exploring the baking world that I had put on hold many years prior.

A few years ago, a pastry chef friend of mine shared some of his sourdough starter with me. At the time I had very little knowledge of how to maintain it properly. After almost killing it a few times, I decided to bake my first loaf of bread at home. It came out so dense and heavy, but being the perfectionist that I am, it made me immediately begin to obsess, wanting to perfect my baking skills. I soon fell back in love with bread and baked goods, the origin of my youthful passion for food. I decided to create an Instagram page called _breadcrumb, a space completely dedicated to my baking where I became part of a fantastic community of fellow bread enthusiasts. Through this process I also found my passion for photography, and I was able to channel that creativity by capturing the images for this book myself.

In each new city I have lived in, the people I have met and the different restaurants that I have experienced over the years have helped me to grow and learn more about myself and the culinary world in a way that I would have never imagined. Cooking and baking allow me to be connected to nature and encourage me to explore the land around me and utilize each ingredient thoughtfully, taking me back to my early days foraging with my grandma. I am always hungry to learn more, to discover new ingredients and techniques and inspire joy for everyone I meet.

I hope this book can awaken this same appetite in you because bread to me is more than just something to be consumed. It's culture, tradition and joy.

getting started

If you're not new to baking, you probably have at your disposal the basics in terms of equipment. However, there are a few key items that I would suggest you invest in that will help you perfect your baking process. I have listed some of the equipment that I find fundamental and worth having in your kitchen, and I wanted to share some of the reasons why I feel they are important. Whether it's about closely monitoring the temperature of your dough or more accurately measuring your ingredients on a digital scale, you want to have these essentials at your disposal.

baker's essentials

digital scale

All the ingredients listed in this book are measured in grams and ounces, including the liquids. A digital scale is the most essential tool that you're going to need in order to get your ingredients ready. Baking requires specific ratios between ingredients, and opting for weight rather than volume allows you to be precise and consistent.

In addition, small variations in the amount of salt or starter can compromise the fermentation process, and by using a scale you are able to measure in smaller, more precise increments. There are plenty of inexpensive scales on the market, but you'll want to make sure you pick one that is easy to read and that ideally weighs ingredients up to 2 kilograms (4.41 lbs).

stand mixer

Incorporating ingredients and mixing by hand gives a tactile connection to the experience that is uniquely satisfying. However, there are times when a stand mixer is an essential tool that facilitates and speeds up the mixing time and allows for better gluten development.

For small batches of dough, I personally mix my preferments and autolyse my flour by hand, and then I transfer the dough into a mixer for the final mix. In this book I have included details on both methods. If you don't own a stand mixer, I would definitely consider investing in one as you will need it to follow the pastry recipes in the book as well as the pizza and focaccia recipes.

digital thermometer

The use of a digital thermometer to monitor the temperature of your ingredients and your final dough is key to a successful bake. You want to make sure that your dough doesn't exceed a temperature of 75°F to 80°F (24°C to 27°C) for optimal gluten development and proofing conditions.

Baking on a hot summer day means that your fermentation will be more active than when you're handling your dough in a colder environment. Make sure you take advantage of a digital thermometer to monitor your ingredients' temperature so you can make the necessary adjustments before you start baking. As you get more comfortable with the process and start understanding your baking environment, you'll soon develop an intuition for things of this nature.

proofing box

There are different ways to proof bread (see page 22 for more on proofing methods). With that being said, for most of my sourdough recipes, after mixing my dough I transfer it to a 10 x 12 x 3–inch (25 x 30 x 7–cm) rectangular plastic tub to bulk proof, especially when making larger quantities. The rectangular shape that the dough relaxes into helps facilitate folding during the bulk fermentation, though a large enough mixing bowl could also be used to proof your dough. Whichever vessel you decide to use, make sure to pick one that will allow for at least a 50% increase in volume.

banneton

Proofing the final shaped loaf in these wooden baskets is the single most popular way to handle dough during the last fermentation stage before baking your bread. For the recipes listed in this book, I suggest you use a 10-inch (25-cm) oval basket. Depending on your preference regarding the look on the surface of your bread, they can be used lined with a cloth or without, but always dusted with flour to prevent it from sticking. If you use a cloth in the banneton, your loaf will absorb the dusted flour evenly, creating a smooth top that allows you to achieve different scoring designs. If you proof directly in the dusted basket, your loaf will absorb the flour captured into the small layer cracks as it relaxes into the banneton, resulting in the traditional floured striped look after baking. If you're just getting started and don't have a banneton available, you may utilize a mixing bowl lined with a cloth dusted with flour.

spray bottle

This is a tool that can be used at different stages of baking. For example, to coat my bread in seeds or cracked grains so that they adhere to the surface evenly, I usually lightly spray my shaped loaves or lay them on a damp towel so that they absorb some moisture. A spray bottle can also be used to spray the inside of your oven to create steam as you load your loaves or to mist your work surface when preshaping and laminating dough. No matter what, having a spray bottle on hand is always useful.

scoring/bread lame

Scoring allows for a more even expansion of the loaf in the first stages of baking, and using a lame will help you slash your loaves more consistently. You might already be using a straight blade to score or simply holding a razor blade. Both work and are effective ways to create intricate patterns and small cuts. However, I would suggest adding a curved bread lame to your scoring tools. The slightly bent metal tip allows you to position the razor blade on a curve, which helps score the dough on an angle, forcing a flap of dough to form. This flap will peel back during the baking process, creating a more pronounced ear in your final baked loaf. There are many types of bread lames available on the market. I prefer the ones with short and slim handles for better control on the cut. If you don't have a razor blade or a bread lame, a sharp paring knife can be used as an alternative.

dutch oven

Baking in a Dutch oven is the preferred method listed in most recipes in this book. Ideally you want to use a pan wide enough to allow for your bread to expand. I prefer to use a cast-iron pan with a shallow bottom and a deep dome cover instead of a deep Dutch oven, as I find it easier to load my bread into it. Remember to always preheat your Dutch oven before placing the loaf in the pan. If you are looking for an alternative to using a Dutch oven, you could bake your bread directly in the oven on a pizza stone with a deep metal tray filled with lava rocks. You will pour water over the hot rocks to create steam in the oven chamber, which will achieve close to the same results. (See more baking techniques on page 29.)

baking stone

A large rectangular baking stone is an essential piece of equipment when making pizza or if you decide you want to bake bread on it instead of using a Dutch oven. The tempered brick material reaches and maintains high temperatures, mimicking the bottom of a pizza oven. This results in a gradual and consistent heat conduction to the bottom of your dough so that the crust and toppings will bake evenly.

pizza peel

If you settled on a pizza stone and you're anxious to make pizza, I suggest you start looking for a pizza peel. Peels are usually built with an aluminum paddle or completely made of wood. I prefer using metal as it's thin enough to easily slide between the pizza and the counter.

grain mill

I have always felt it is extremely important to support my local farmers and mills through my sourcing of fresh ingredients. As you advance through your baking journey and explore different grains, you might want to consider investing in your own grain mill. Not only does it give you the power to create your own mix of flour, but by using whole local grains at the height of their nutritional peak, your bread will reach depths of flavor that are otherwise impossible to achieve. In my opinion, this is definitely a tool to consider investing in.

ingredients

wheat

Bread is made with a few essential elements, though flour is the one component that ultimately determines the unique and distinct flavor of your final baked product. That being said, we can't talk about bread and flour if we don't highlight the role that different grains play in bread making.

Common wheat is the variety most cultivated across the globe, and it's primarily classified by its growing season. The two types are **winter wheat** and **spring wheat**. Winter wheat is planted in the fall, goes dormant over the winter and is harvested in summer, while spring wheat is planted in spring and harvested in late summer to early fall.

Additionally, we can divide wheat into two categories: **hard wheat** and **soft wheat**. Both are identified by the color of the kernel, which can be red or white. Hard red wheat usually has a higher protein content and is mostly employed to make rustic artisan bread. The nutritional composition of the two is similar and the hard white was developed by eliminating the genes for the bran color while preserving the characteristics of red wheat, and it usually contains a slightly lower protein percentage. They differ in flavor as the hard red develops nuttier and more bitter notes, while the white has a milder and sweeter taste.

Soft wheat, compared to the hard varieties, has a significantly lower protein content and it is best employed to make pastries and softer breads. The two types are also combined to make different kinds of flours, like all-purpose flour, which is made with approximately 80% hard wheat and 20% soft, depending on the brand.

In the recipes of this book, I will specify the types of grains used in each bread. You will find high-protein wheat flour and whole wheat flour used for most of my breads. High-protein flour is usually made with a hard wheat and includes all those flours that contain a protein percentage above 12%. This is a flour that absorbs more water than, for example, a soft pastry flour (8 to 9% protein) and all-purpose flour (10 to 12% protein), resulting in a stronger and more elastic dough that will better trap gases during fermentation and develop an open crumb and thicker crust in your breads.

Whole wheat flour is also made from hard wheat and also has a high protein content. It's darker in color because a portion or all of the germ and bran are left in it and not sifted out after the milling process, which makes this kind of flour more nutritious and richer in flavor. I personally almost always add a percentage of whole wheat flour to my breads and a small amount to my pizza dough (5 to 10%) to improve their flavor and overall texture. **Keep in mind that the protein percentage in flour varies among types of wheat and their growing conditions as well as processing methods**, mainly milling, which determines the amount of germ left in the flour, its nutritional value and characteristics of a specific flour.

Besides common wheat and other grains like rye, durum wheat or semolina and barley, we'll also be exploring ancient grains in this book. This category includes spelt, einkorn, khorasan and emmer/farro, which are grains that belong in the wheat family. They are classified as ancient because they have been unchanged over the course of the past several hundred and thousand years. Other heirloom varieties of common grains, like black barley, teff, quinoa, millet, amaranth, red rice and blue corn, are also ancient grains.

spelt

This grain can be considered emmer and einkorn's cousin. It's higher in protein than common wheat, and the gluten in this grain develops a more extensible dough that will give your spelt bread greater volume. From a flavor perspective, this delicious grain develops mild nutty notes with a sweeter taste. Spelt can also be a healthier choice because it is more water soluble than common wheat, making it easier to digest.

emmer/farro

This grain is closely related to spelt and einkorn. It has a delicate gluten and is high in protein, which makes it among the most nutritious and versatile grains. I like to source whole emmer wheat berries and mill them myself because I think this grain in particular expresses its best characteristics when freshly milled. Bluebird emmer flour is among my favorite brands, and when I mill it fresh I often add a percentage to many of my breads to develop a rich and unique flavor profile.

einkorn

This grain is known as the oldest variety of wheat. This particular species of grass grew wild for thousands of years before it was cultivated. It has a more delicate gluten and a silky texture. The weaker gluten makes it easier to digest, and it can be enjoyed by many people who otherwise could not consume common wheat. The flavor that einkorn develops is grassy and toasted and creates a distinct crunchy crust with a soft yellowish crumb.

khorasan

This wheat has a large and elongated golden-colored kernel. It's higher in protein and more nutritious than common wheat, and the bread made using khorasan flour develops a soft and chewy crumb, with a deep buttery and sweet flavor. Adding a percentage of khorasan to your breads (up to 60%) will elevate the overall bake, improving texture and flavor and allowing you to work with high-hydration doughs as this flour absorbs a large amount of water.

local ingredients

As a trained chef, I'm interested in ingredients and their quality just as much as I enjoy creating with them. Each grain offers very unique characteristics that impact textures, density and flavor in the final baked product. In order to achieve the result I desire, I first look to local mills. I find that by directly sourcing from the people most closely connected with the grain, I'm able to get a more accurate understanding of the qualities expressed in each one.

Some of the brands I have been working with include Central Milling, King Arthur, Jovial Foods, Bench View Farms and Bluebird Grain Farms, where I source a wide variety of organic flours, from high-protein and all-purpose flour to specialty flours and ancient grains as well as whole wheat berries that I use in most of my breads. Some of the brands I use for pizza include Polselli, Molino Pasini and Caputo.

I suggest that everyone seek out local ingredients, as this type of connection to the land and what it produces only serves to enhance the quality of your final product. Note that if one specific brand of flour doesn't yield the result you desire after a few bakes, I suggest switching brands and experimenting with different grains. You will notice a drastic change by replacing the flour in a recipe, which will ultimately allow you to develop different flavor profiles, crumb structure and texture in your bread.

Exploring the endless combinations and what each grain has to offer is a never-ending journey, and in this book I want to guide you through the differences in each grain and show you how I utilize them to make delicious and beautiful bread by including some unusual combinations.

As you get familiar with the different kinds of flours, you can aim to achieve the result you desire by sourcing various grains and creating your own mix.

Now that we have explored the different grains and their characteristics, I want to highlight the function and importance of the different essential ingredients used when baking bread.

water

The importance of water as an ingredient should not be underestimated because water has different functions in baking. It hydrates the flour in the mix, allowing your dough to develop the right consistency and creating the perfect environment for yeast to ferment. It not only hydrates the flour, but also helps disperse ingredients like salt and yeast in the dough and provides an extra source of nutrition for those yeasts thanks to minerals like calcium and magnesium present in water. For that reason, my personal preference is to use natural spring water when I can; tap water and some purified water brands may contain low levels of chlorine, which can inhibit fermentation.

Many home bakers find that their tap water is just fine for baking, but if you have any issues with your baking, then don't rule out the water as a potential factor. Using spring mineral water eliminates this as a variable that may adversely affect your baked goods.

For most of my sourdough bread recipes, I use room temperature water (70°F [21°C]), but depending on your environment, you should adjust the temperature of your water before adding it to the mix. In a warmer environment, you'll want to use cooler water and vice versa. However, starting with slightly colder water (50°F to 60°F [10°C to 15°C]) will help your dough maintain a lower temperature during mixing, which allows you to extend the mixing time for better gluten development, especially when using a small stand mixer and working with high hydration doughs.

salt

Flavor enhancement is probably what comes to mind when you think of salt in leavened products, even though there are some breads I grew up eating in Italy like Pane Sciocco and Sciapo that are made without salt to carry on the tradition and cater to the preferences of the regions in which they are made. These days, the salt selection in my kitchen cabinet varies from type of salt and place of origin. From Maldon to Cervia, Sicilian, Murray River, fleur de sel, Himalayan, kosher and sea salt—I love to use them all in different preparations for their distinct characteristics.

You're probably wondering, which one should I use to make bread? And when should I add it to my dough? Well, when it comes to sprinkling salt on focaccia right before baking, I say get creative and use your favorite salt, but in your bread dough I suggest you use noniodized fine sea salt.

There are many theories that debate when salt should be added to the mix, and ultimately there is no right or wrong way to incorporate salt into your dough. Whether salt is added at the beginning stages of mixing or after gluten has formed is completely up to the baker.

Salt has many functions. It not only adds flavor but also has an osmotic effect on the dough, which simply put means it draws moisture from the mix. **The result of this osmotic reaction affects flavor and rise by regulating the yeast activity as it inhibits fermentation.** Salt also plays a role in gluten development. When added at the beginning stages of mixing, it causes flour to hydrate more slowly, creating a more tenacious interaction between proteins and resulting in a stronger dough.

The reason why many bakers choose to incorporate salt at the end of the mix, after gluten has already formed, is to make sure not to alter the characteristics of the dough and to keep a consistent product. This is also a step employed when using the autolyse technique (page 21) because salt slows down the enzymatic activity that happens during the rest period.

I have found that I can keep a consistent bake when I add salt to my dough after gluten has formed. So for the majority of the sourdough recipes in this book, salt is added at the end of the mix, unless specified otherwise.

sourdough starter

The foundation of bread making lies in the ability to manage the process of fermentation. **Sourdough starter is in fact a mixture of fermented flour and water that, when combined and maintained over time, creates the perfect environment for natural yeast and bacteria to grow and thrive.** By feeding (or refreshing) this culture regularly with fresh flour and water, we "train" the culture into producing a vigorous activity in the mixture that ultimately will be the vehicle that leavens our dough. Sourdough starter also creates the distinct sour and acidic flavor profile in our bread thanks to the lactic acid and acetic acid produced during fermentation. **Time and temperature play a fundamental role in the activity and life of a sourdough culture.** The temperature at which the sourdough starter is stored as well as its hydration will determine its activity as microorganisms thrive in a warmer and wetter environment (see more on how to make and maintain your starter on page 19).

baker's yeast or fresh yeast

This texturally soft and crumbly yeast is usually sold in small blocks and is composed entirely of living cells. It is perishable and should be refrigerated. I personally prefer to use this type of yeast for the distinct flavor that it infuses and because it is, in my opinion, the most reliable kind of yeast when baking, especially when employed in long fermentations like pizza, focaccia and croissant doughs.

This kind of commercial yeast can be incorporated into the mix by being dissolved in liquids or added directly to the dry ingredients.

To convert from fresh yeast to dry, I generally use half the amount of active dry yeast and one-third of the amount of instant yeast called for in the recipe.

active dry yeast and instant dry yeast

These kinds of granular dry yeast are living organisms that are dormant until activated and incorporated into your dough. They both function as a leavening agent but differ from each other in the way you incorporate each one into your mix. They can be used interchangeably, but something to consider is that for active dry yeast you should use 25% more than the instant dry yeast.

Active dry yeast is probably what comes to mind when you think of yeast—and it's the most common variety sold in grocery stores. You must activate this kind by dissolving it in lukewarm water (or another liquid) called for in a recipe at a temperature of 110°F (43°C) before adding it to your dough. Instant dry yeast can be added directly into the dry ingredients without the need to be hydrated.

biga and poolish

Biga and poolish are the Italian and French terms, respectively, that describe a preferment.

They are simply a portion of the dough (usually containing 30 to 50% of the total flour) mixed and proofed in advance, sometime up to 16 hours before mixing the final dough.

Just like sourdough starter, they function as a leavening agent. However, they do differ from sourdough by the kind of yeast they contain, as a sourdough starter is a culture of natural yeast and biga and poolish are made with commercial yeast, either fresh or dry.

Preferments are employed by bakers to manage the fermentation process as well as to improve the structure of a dough and subsequently to build texture and flavor in the final baked product. The small amount of yeast that is left to ferment in the dough for a long period of time infuses flavor by fermenting sugars and producing alcohol and carbon dioxide as byproducts. Those two preferments are both made with flour, water and a small amount of yeast, as low as 0.1% of the flour weight.

start your own sourdough culture

As mentioned earlier, when we use sourdough starter as our leavening agent, we are manipulating a living culture of microorganisms that requires attention and care.

After creating the perfect environment for natural yeast and bacteria to grow and thrive, the three fundamental elements to consider when handling your starter are time, temperature and hydration. Besides that, all you really have to worry about is to periodically feed (or refresh) the culture with fresh flour and water to keep it alive and active.

To create your sourdough starter, use a small percentage of rye flour, as this is an extremely nutritious grain and it will help you expedite the fermentation process. If you don't have rye flour, a good-quality organic whole wheat flour will also work well.

100 g (3.53 oz) sourdough starter culture

to start your culture

10 g (0.35 oz) rye flour

40 g (1.41 oz) high-protein wheat flour

50 g (1.76 oz) water

In a small mixing bowl, combine the flours and the water, preferably at 90°F (32°C). Stir them together until the flour is fully hydrated. Then transfer the mixture into a glass jar and cover it with either a loose lid or a damp cloth held with a rubber band.

Let the jar sit, preferably at a temperature between 70°F and 80°F (21°C and 26°C), for 24 hours. If you're starting this process in a cool environment and your kitchen temperature is below 70°F (21°C), I suggest you turn your oven light on and keep the jar inside the oven, as the chamber will heat up just enough to create the perfect environment for yeast and bacteria to grow. Otherwise, a kitchen counter close to a stovetop is probably the best spot for it.

The next day, weigh 50 grams (1.76 oz) of the mixture (discard the rest) and 50 grams (1.76 oz) of water into a mixing bowl, add 40 grams (1.41 oz) of bread flour and 10 grams (0.35 oz) of rye flour and stir thoroughly. Transfer the mixture again into a clean glass jar and let it sit for another 24 hours.

Repeat feeding your culture once a day every 24 hours for the first 5 days. Most likely you won't see any activity in the starter for the first 3 to 4 days. After day 5 and onward, start feeding your starter twice a day, every 12 hours, with the same ratio of flour and water for at least 20 to 30 days.

From this point forward, your culture should be active enough to be used and you may proceed with feeding your starter high-protein wheat flour only. I suggest experimenting by adding a percentage of different types of flour, like rye, for example, when you build a levain to create a unique flavor profile in your final baked loaf.

At this stage you may also store the starter in the refrigerator for up to a few months without feeding it. However, although it is very resilient, if your sourdough starter is just a few months old, I suggest feeding and refreshing it every 7 to 10 days if kept in the refrigerator. I also suggest you take your starter out of the fridge and let it go through at least one feeding cycle before you bake with it.

(continued)

After about a month, you should be able to predict the rise and fall of your starter. At its peak, the volume should triple in size, and once it has passed the sweet spot it will start deflating. I encourage you to keep track of its growth over time and mark the jar as it rises so that you can have a better understanding of its behavior and know exactly how long it takes for it to reach peak. There are a few variables that impact the activity of your culture. The most critical to consider is temperature.

It's fundamental to understand the balance between time and temperature to be able to successfully predict the growth of your sourdough starter. In a warmer environment (above 75°F [24°C]), your starter will reach peak rapidly, whereas if it is kept cool (below 70° [21°C]), its activity will slow down significantly. Note that a sourdough starter fed with equal parts water and flour kept at a sweet spot between 70°F and 75°F (21°C and 24°C) should reach peak in 3 to 4 hours if it is healthy and strong.

Other important factors that impact the activity of your culture are the hydration and the kind of flour you use to feed it. A starter that is refreshed with a lower percentage of water will take longer to mature and reach peak, which allows you to control the fermentation time and schedule exactly when to mix the final dough. The sourdough starter we created earlier is considered a young or liquid starter or 100% hydration, meaning it's refreshed with equal parts starter, water and flour. This can also be expressed as a 1:1:1 ratio, which indicates the proportion between starter, water and flour respectively. As you get more comfortable with managing the fermentation, you can manipulate the activity of the culture by lowering the hydration.

One way to test the readiness of your starter is by performing a float test. Fill up a mixing bowl or a container with water and pour in a spoonful of starter. If it floats it's ready to be used. Note that an overfermented starter will still float, but you can notice the difference in the texture as the overfermented starter will be stringy with a loose, batter-like consistency. What you're looking for in your starter is some strength and the consistency of a thick bubbly batter that will stay together in a clump when floating. Depending on the ratios of different flours you feed your starter with, you'll see how your bread will change in flavor and texture, so the kind of flour you decide to use is completely up to your preference.

master sourdough method

In this section I'm going to walk you through the details of each step of my sourdough bread–making process. My goal is to equip you with the basics that you will need to achieve the best results when baking the bread recipes listed in this book. From building your levain to mixing, proofing, shaping and baking your bread, whether this is new territory for you or you're looking for inspiration, I'd like to guide you in your baking journey.

build a levain

Levain is the French word that describes sourdough starter. In fact the two are essentially the same thing. Once your starter is active and you're able to predict its rise and fall, when it reaches peak you can either use it directly to mix your dough or feed it a specific amount to build a levain. **This is a way to portion and preferment a specific amount of flour in a formula.** As mentioned earlier, a levain with a lower hydration will take longer to rise and reach peak and vice versa. So the percentage of mature starter can be fed with a different ratio of water and flour to best suit your schedule.

A levain is also a great way to develop a specific flavor profile in your bread, as you can utilize different flours to feed it without impacting your main starter. The levain I use in the recipes listed in this book vary from hydration to ratios of flour because every levain is built for each specific bread. You will also find that for many breads I simply list mature starter among the ingredients, which means you should use your liquid 100% hydration sourdough starter.

autolyse

This is a step where you simply combine the flour with some or all of the water in a recipe and then leave the mixture to rest at room temperature or in the refrigerator for a period of time that could vary from a minimum of 15 to 20 minutes to as long as overnight (8 to 12 hours). For each recipe listed in this book, I suggest a specific length of autolyse; however, you may choose to shorten or lengthen this step based on your schedule and your levain fermentation. Keep in mind that a longer autolyse will improve your dough structure and build greater flavor.

During autolyse I always keep the dough covered with a damp towel or wrap the bowl with plastic wrap to control moisture and prevent the surface from drying out. If your environment temperature is above 80°F (26°C), I suggest you autolyse your water and flour in the refrigerator for at least 30 minutes before incorporating your levain into the dough. This will allow your dough to cool down and not overheat during mixing.

Auto-lysis means self-digestion. In fact, during this process of hydrating the flour, the enzymes contained in it begin breaking down proteins and start to form gluten bonds, increasing the dough extensibility. This reduces the mixing time significantly and helps create a stronger gluten structure, resulting in a more elastic and tenacious dough. Ultimately the elasticity is what allows the dough to trap gaseous byproducts produced during fermentation, resulting in a more airy and light dough.

I have found this step extremely useful in some of my bakes, and the sweet spot of autolyse in my dough is usually between 1 and 2 hours.

mix

After the autolyse, your dough is ready for the mature starter or levain to be incorporated.

Make sure you factor in the time your levain needs to reach its peak so that it will coincide with the time you autolyse your flour. Remember that autolyse helps create better structure and improves flavor in your dough but is not an absolutely necessary step. If your starter or levain is ready and you're only one-third or halfway through your autolyse, just mix your mature starter or levain in and don't let it overferment.

However, if you mix by hand, I suggest you autolyse your dough for at least 30 minutes. The preferred mixing method for the recipes listed in this book is with the use of a stand mixer, but I also wanted to include a hand mixing technique.

Using a stand mixer fitted with the dough hook attachment, add the mature starter or levain to your autolysed dough and mix it on low (speed 2) for 3 minutes. Increase the speed to medium-high (speed 6) and keep mixing for 5 to 8 minutes. The dough should gain strength at this point and develop elasticity, pulling from the sides of the bowl. Reduce the speed back to low (speed 2) and add the salt. This step will take only 2 minutes. Once the salt is fully incorporated, the dough should be smooth and feel tight. Turn the machine off, cover the mixing bowl with a towel or plastic wrap and let the dough rest for at least 15 minutes before taking it out of the bowl. This resting period will allow the gluten to relax after it has tightened during the mechanical force applied during the length of mixing.

One important element to keep in mind while mixing is the temperature of your dough, which at the end of the mix should not exceed 78°F to 80°F (25°C to 26°C). Adding cooler water to the mix helps keep the temperature down. **I suggest taking the temperature of your water down to at least 50°F to 60°F (10°C to 15°C)** before mixing by chilling it in the refrigerator for a few hours or by adding ice cubes to it before measuring the amount needed. Starting with cold water will help you maintain a final dough temperature between the range indicated above, especially when baking in summer or in a hot environment. **However, I suggest you use a digital thermometer to monitor the temperature of your ingredients and your final dough** to have a better understanding of what temperature water you should be using before mixing, which will ultimately help you develop an intuition for things of this nature. You want to make sure not to overheat the dough to avoid compromising the gluten development.

Have a proofing box ready that is big enough to hold the dough, preferably of rectangular shape. Keep in mind that the dough will increase in volume by 30 to 50%. At this point the dough should be elastic and not excessively sticky. Wet your hands with water, scoop the dough up in a circular motion from the bowl and quickly fold it into itself a few times to tighten it lightly before transferring it to the proofing box.

If you decide to mix by hand, incorporate your mature starter or levain into the autolysed dough by pinching and turning the dough into itself until the mature starter or levain is completely absorbed. This step will take 5 to 10 minutes. Let the dough rest for 30 minutes, covered with a towel or plastic wrap, then proceed with adding the salt. Keep mixing by pulling and folding the dough into itself until it starts gaining some strength. This process should take another 5 to 10 minutes. Don't worry if the dough doesn't seem to be perfectly smooth at this stage—throughout the bulk proof fermentation it will gain strength as you perform sets of folds.

Transfer the dough into a proofing box or leave it in the mixing bowl and start the bulk proof fermentation, making sure you keep your box covered and preferably at a temperature between 75°F and 80°F (23°C and 26°C).

bulk proof

The bulk proof of a dough is the fermentation of the whole mass before dividing and preshaping as needed into what will become a loaf. **It is fundamental that you control the temperature and humidity at this stage, as this will determine how fast and well your dough will rise.** I have found that a very consistent method would be to turn your oven into a proofing chamber with a few simple steps.

Turn your oven light on at least 30 minutes before placing your dough in it. This will slowly increase the temperature in the chamber as the lightbulb heats up, creating the perfect environment for your dough to rise. For humidity control, I found that by simply placing a container with approximately 1 kilogram (35 oz) of hot water (it should be 130°F [55°C]) on the bottom rack of my oven, the steam produced will increase and hold the humidity in the chamber to 70 to 80%. Make sure you place the warm water into the oven in advance so that the humidity will rise in the chamber before you add the dough. You may keep the dough uncovered during bulk fermentation thanks to the high humidity level, which will allow your dough to stay moist, preventing it from drying during the bulk proof. Replenish or reheat the water periodically as it cools down during the length of the bulk fermentation to maintain a humidity level above 70%. I find this method to be more efficient than proofing dough at room temperature because humidity, as well as temperature, is a fundamental factor that helps promote fermentation.

I suggest you use this method for proofing all of the breads in this book as well as your poolish or biga. If you're looking to monitor exactly the temperature and humidity of your proofing chamber, I strongly recommend the use of a digital hygrometer.

I typically bulk proof my dough for 4 to 6 hours at a temperature between 75°F and 80°F (24°C and 26°C), performing sets of folds. Depending on the recipe, I may use lamination.

lamination

Laminating consists of stretching the dough into a thin layer on a damp countertop (previously sprayed with water) by pulling it outward possibly in a rectangular shape and then folding it back up into itself (here is where a spray bottle comes in handy). I employ this technique to combine different color doughs to create a marbled effect as well as to sometimes incorporate seeds and other inclusions. This technique is also a great way to increase the dough's strength, but not a necessary one. You may choose to skip this step and add inclusions directly to your dough while performing folds during the bulk fermentation. If you decide to incorporate seeds and other ingredients to your dough using lamination, I suggest you proceed with laminating after the first 45 minutes to 1 hour of your dough's bulk proof, and then keep proofing the dough and performing regular sets of folds as indicated in each recipe. When combining different color doughs together, I prefer bulk proofing the two doughs separately and then laminating and combining them toward the end of the bulk proof. This way I can maintain a clearer marbled effect between the two doughs, preserving the contrast between the two colors, whereas if I were to laminate and combine the two doughs at the beginning of the bulk proof, the different colors would meld together while performing sets of folds during the bulk fermentation.

the lamination process step by step

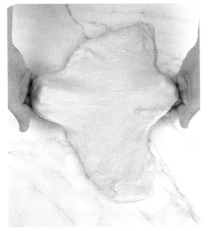

Stretch and enlarge the dough into a rectangular shape onto a wet countertop surface.

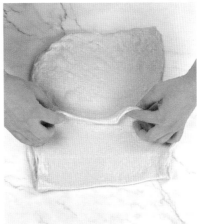

Fold one-third of the dough over the center.

Fold the last third of the dough over the center.

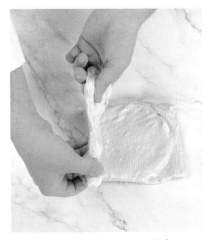

Pull and fold the dough over one-third of the rectangle.

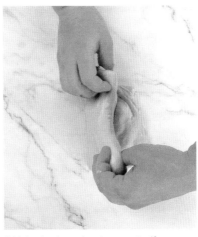

Fold the dough one last time onto itself.

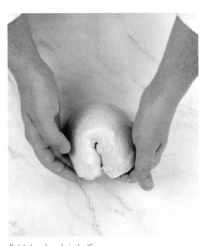

Fold the dough in half.

the bi-color lamination process step by step

Place both doughs next to each other onto a wet countertop surface.

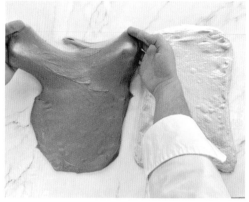

Stretch and enlarge the doughs into a rectangular shape.

Make sure both doughs are the same size.

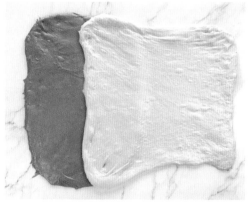

Pull half of the white dough onto half of the purple.

Fold the purple dough over and onto the overlapped white half.

Fold the last white half over and onto the purple one.

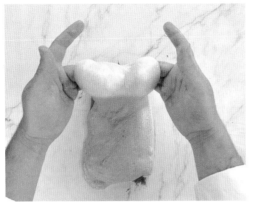

Starting from the side farthest from you, pull and stretch the dough upwards and toward yourself.

Proceed folding the dough over and underneath itself.

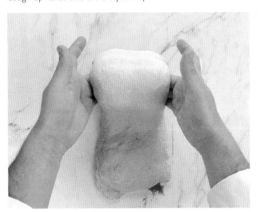

Continue pulling the dough.

Keep folding and tucking the dough.

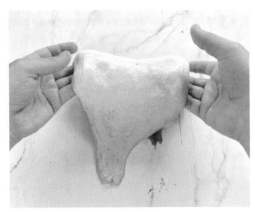

Repeat pulling and folding the dough.

Fold and roll the dough until the seam is left underneath.

the coil fold process step by step

Pull and stretch one side of the dough upward and fold it onto iself.

Repeat with the opposite side.

The dough should be evenly folded on both sides.

Proceed pulling and folding one side of the dough.

Repeat with the opposite side.

The dough should again be evenly folded.

stretch and fold and coil fold

During the length of the bulk proof fermentation, you want to make sure you perform folds to build strength and improve the structure of your dough. The two methods used are a stretch and fold and a coil fold.

These two techniques of folding the dough differ from each other by the way the fold is performed. In the stretch and fold, one side of the dough is pulled and stretched repeatedly over the top of the dough until the entire mass is folded onto itself. This method is usually employed for larger quantities of dough as it would be hard to pick up a heavy dough and fold it over itself. A coil fold is a gentler way to fold, as this method uses gravity as the stretching force and is the preferred method used in all recipes listed in this book.

As mentioned earlier, I suggest you bulk proof your dough using a rectangular-shaped container, either plastic or glass, as this will facilitate folding. While bulk proofing your dough, begin performing the first set of folds after 45 minutes to 1 hour and repeat this step throughout the length of bulk fermentation as indicated in each recipe.

After the first 45 minutes to 1 hour of bulk fermentation, your dough will have relaxed into the shape of your proofing vessel, and at this stage it will feel tenacious. Starting from one side of the dough, wet your hands and then pick it up from the center and pull it upward. As gravity stretches it, fold the one side over and onto itself. Repeat with the opposite side and then proceed with folding the two remaining sides by picking up each one and folding the dough into itself.

As you keep performing folds every 45 minutes to 1 hour (or as specified in each recipe), your dough elasticity will improve as it will slowly inflate and feel softer. This will facilitate performing the remaining sets of folds needed during the bulk fermentation.

If performing lamination after the first 45 minutes to 1 hour of the bulk fermentation, you may skip the first set of folds as lamination will replace this step. Keep performing sets of folds 45 minutes to 1 hour after laminating your dough or as specified in each recipe.

I typically perform no more than four sets of folds during my bulk proof before preshaping and getting my dough ready to be shaped. **Always consider temperature as a key factor in your bulk fermentation; proofing in a warmer environment will affect the time it takes for your dough to rise, speeding up the process, and vice versa.**

preshape and bench rest

This step consists of dividing and portioning your dough after the bulk proof to get the loaves ready to be shaped.

After your bulk proof, flip the proofing box onto a lightly floured surface and let the proofed dough ease out of the container and onto the counter. With the help of a bench knife, divide the dough into two loaves, or as indicated in each recipe, and preshape it into round balls. Roll and tuck the dough into itself just enough to create some tension, carefully trying not to rip the surface. Dust the top of the preshaped dough with flour and transfer it back into the proofing box or a mixing bowl. Let the dough rest, uncovered, in a proofing chamber (page 22) or covered with plastic wrap at room temperature, as indicated in each recipe.

the preshape process step by step

Transfer your dough onto a lightly floured surface.

With a bench knife positioned at a 45° angle, start rolling the dough.

Keep rolling in a circular motion.

Tuck the dough underneath and into itself as you roll.

Continue rolling and pulling the dough toward yourself to tighten the ball.

The pre-shaped dough should be tight and look smooth and even.

shaping a batard

Pull and fold one-third of the dough over the center.

Repeat with the opposite side.

Pull and fold the top over the center.

Start rolling the dough toward yourself.

Tuck the dough underneath with your thumbs as you roll it.

Keep rolling the dough until the seam is left underneath.

Pinch the sides of the shaped loaf to seal the edges.

Transfer the shaped loaf into a proofing basket seam side up.

shape

What's fascinating about shaping bread is that no matter how consistent you try to be, no two loaves of bread will ever look exactly the same. There are many ways you can shape, and each technique will result in a different crumb structure in your bread. For the majority of the recipes listed in this book, the preferred method uses the batard shaping technique, but I have also included details on how to shape a boule and a simple loaf.

While your preshaped loaves are resting, get your banneton baskets ready and dusted with flour. I suggest for all recipes listed in this book that you use a 10-inch (25-cm) oval basket unless otherwise specified. After it has been preshaped and rested, flip the dough top side down from the proofing container onto a lightly floured surface, where your dough will relax into a round shape.

For shaping a batard, stretch by pulling one side with both hands and folding it over the center onto one-third of the round. Pull and stretch the opposite side and fold it by overlapping it over the opposite folded side. Pull the top down over the center and roll down toward you until the seam is left underneath. Pinch the seams on both ends of the loaf to seal and transfer the shaped loaf seam side up into the banneton basket. Cover the basket with a kitchen towel to get it ready for the final proof. (See images on page 28.)

For shaping a boule, flip the preshaped dough top side down from the proofing container onto a lightly floured surface, where your dough will relax into a round shape. Pull and fold the outer edges toward the center one at a time, turning the dough 90 degrees once each folded side sticks and seals to the center. Repeat until you have folded all the edges to the center of the round, then flip the dough so that it is sitting on the folded sides. Using both hands, roll the dough, giving it a round shape to tuck and seal the bottom. Transfer the shaped loaf into a 10-inch (25-cm) round banneton, top side down, and cover it with a towel to get it ready for the final proof. (See images on page 30.)

For shaping a simple loaf, flip the preshaped dough top side down onto a lightly floured surface, where your dough will relax into a round shape. Starting with the outer ends, pull and stretch both sides simultaneously outward and fold them so the edges meet in the center of the dough. Using both hands, pull the top and fold it one-third over the center of the rectangle. Keep rolling and pressing the top down and over the folded side with both hands until the seam side is left underneath. Pinch the sides of the shaped loaf to seal the edges. (See images on page 31.)

final proof

Once your dough is shaped and in the banneton basket, you have two options: let the shaped loaf final proof at room temperature for 3 hours before baking or place the basket in the fridge to slow down and extend fermentation. The majority of bread I bake uses the second method, though you always have the option to use the first method if you are baking your loaf all in one day. Right after shaping I usually place my banneton in the fridge overnight for a maximum of 14 to 16 hours to cold proof. Extending the bulk fermentation is essential to build flavor in your bread as the cold temperature significantly slows down the enzymatic activity, resulting in the development of a more complex flavor.

score and bake

Your bread is finally ready to be baked. The preferred method I employ in most sourdough breads in this book requires the use of a Dutch oven. Preheat your Dutch oven as indicated in each recipe at least 40 minutes in advance. If you are baking bread after a cold proof, pull the basket out of the fridge and flip the loaf from the basket onto a cut-out piece of parchment paper. Score the top and transfer the loaf into the preheated Dutch oven. Place the lid on and bake the loaf as indicated in each recipe.

If you don't have a Dutch oven, there are a few alternatives to successfully bake your bread, which include the use of a pizza stone. When opting to bake directly in the oven, you want to create enough steam in the chamber as you load your loaves so that you can achieve a great oven spring and a thick and rustic crust. To do so, place a deep metal pan filled with lava rocks at the very bottom of the oven and position the pizza stone on the rack level right above the rocks. Preheat the pizza stone and the lava rocks as indicated in each recipe.

Flip the loaf from the banneton onto a cut-out piece of parchment paper, slide a pizza peel or a sheet pan without edges underneath the paper and transfer the loaf onto the preheated pizza stone. As soon as you load the loaf in the oven, pour a half pint (240 ml) of water onto the hot rocks and quickly shut the oven door to create continuous steam. If you don't have lava rocks, simply pour a pint (8.82 oz) of ice cubes into a preheated metal pan.

Bake the loaf with the door shut for at least 20 minutes, then crack the door open just a few inches to release the steam for a few seconds, close the door back up and keep baking following the temperatures indicated in each recipe.

After your bread is baked, transfer it to a wide rack and allow it to cool for at least 30 minutes to 1 hour before cutting into it. When bread comes out of the oven, it still retains a great amount of moisture inside, which keeps baking and pushing the moisture outward until it is cool and set.

shaping a boule

Transfer your dough onto a lightly floured surface and begin folding the edges over the center.

Proceed folding the next side by pulling the corner that formed in the previous fold to the center.

Pull the next corner that formed and fold again over the center.

Make sure to gently press as you fold to seal the dough over the center of the round.

Keep turning the dough and folding the next side over the center.

Make sure all sides are folded and sealed over the center before turning the dough over.

Flip the dough over, folded sides down.

With both hands gently roll the shaped loaf to tighten into a ball shape.

The shaped loaf should be tight and look smooth. Make sure not to roll it excessively to avoid ripping the surface.

shaping a simple loaf

On a lightly floured surface, enlarge the dough into a rectangular shape.

Stretch and fold both sides simultaneously to meet over the center.

Pull and fold the top over and onto a third of the dough, toward yourself.

Firmly press the edge of the folded side down with your finger to seal it onto the dough.

Using your fingers, roll the folded side toward yourself and press down to seal.

Repeat rolling and pressing the dough until the seam is left underneath.

Pinch the sides of the shaped loaf to seal the edges.

Classic and Ancient Grains

When I think of a classic loaf, I'm transported back to Italy. I grew up eating a dark and crusty sourdough bread called Casareccio Romano (page 35), which is a specialty in Rome. Often it accompanied a meal, or it would be used to make my sandwich to pack for lunch at school. In this chapter, I introduce you to another classic from my childhood, ciabatta, which I have modified into a Whole Grain Ciabatta (page 40) that brings an elevated layer of flavor and texture. I also wanted to include recipes such as the Country Loaf (page 39) because this bread formula is easily adaptable, allowing you to experiment with different grains.

In this chapter, we will also explore the use of ancient grains. When I taught myself to bake bread, experimenting with ancient grains helped me to learn about the distinct differences in each one. Their varying flavor and characteristics can impact your overall bake, and I'm happy to share some of that knowledge here with you. Later in the book, you will see how I often introduce small amounts of ancient grains into a recipe to enhance the flavor profile. My goal is to equip you with an understanding of these grains so that as you experiment on your own, you will become comfortable with adding them to your own creations and confident in your ability to achieve unique and successful results.

casareccio romano

Casareccio literally means "home made." Originally made in a small town on the outskirts of Rome, this is the bread that you find in every home in the region and is the bread that takes me back to the comfort food of my roots. The traditional bread is coated in wheat bran and baked in wood-fired ovens at temperatures up to 600°F (315°C), which creates the distinct dark and thick crust. I find that by extending the fermentation time in this recipe, I can achieve a great amount of acidity, and by baking it in a cast-iron Dutch oven for a few minutes longer than usual, the loaf develops an extra thick crust typical of the bread I grew up eating. I also don't score this bread in order to maintain the smooth crust traditional of this loaf. Leavened with natural yeast and mixed with only white flour, this bread is extra crusty and fragrant with a soft and chewy crumb.

yield: 2 loaves

levain

80 g (2.82 oz) high-protein wheat flour

80 g (2.82 oz) water

40 g (1.41 oz) mature starter

final mix

750 g (26.46 oz) high-protein wheat flour

150 g (5.29 oz) all-purpose flour

650 g (22.93 oz) water

200 g (7.05 oz) levain

25 g (0.88 oz) salt

Wheat bran, for coating

Start by building the levain 6 to 8 hours before mixing. For more details on my sourdough method, see page 21.

For the final mix, during the last 60 to 90 minutes of the levain's fermentation, start the autolyse. In the bowl of a stand mixer fitted with the paddle attachment, combine the high-protein wheat flour, all-purpose flour and water until the flour is fully hydrated and there are no dry bits left. This should take no more than 2 minutes. Cover the bowl with a towel or plastic wrap and let the mixture sit at room temperature until the levain reaches peak.

Add your mature levain to the autolysed dough and, using a stand mixer fitted with the dough hook attachment, mix on low (speed 2) for 3 minutes. Increase the speed to medium-high (speed 5) and keep mixing for 5 to 8 minutes, or until the dough has gained strength and is smooth and elastic. Reduce the speed back to low (speed 2) and add the salt, let it incorporate for 2 minutes, then turn the mixer off, cover the bowl with a towel and let the dough rest for 15 minutes in the machine before taking it out.

Place your dough into a proofing box and start the bulk proof at a temperature between 75°F and 80°F (23°C and 26°C) for 5 hours, performing four sets of coil folds, once every hour. Transfer your dough onto a lightly floured surface, divide it into two equal loaves and give each half a rectangular shape with rounded corners by gently stretching each half. Proceed with shaping a simple loaf (page 29).

Dust two 12-inch (30-cm) oval bannetons with finely ground wheat bran and line a shallow tray also filled with finely ground wheat bran. I usually blend the bran to a semolina-like texture so that it will form a more even and smooth layer on the loaf, resulting in a thicker and darker crust typical of this Roman bread. Lightly spray the top of the shaped loaves with water before rolling each one onto the tray. Transfer each loaf into a banneton, seam side up, and place it in the refrigerator, covered with a towel, for the final proof at 39°F (3.9°C) for 12 to 16 hours. I suggest you extend your final proofing time to develop the extra acidity needed to emulate the classic flavor.

Preheat your Dutch oven to 500°F (260°C), line it with a piece of parchment paper and place the proofed loaf in the Dutch oven. Bake it with the lid on at 500°F (260°C) for 5 minutes, then drop the temperature to 480°F (248°C) and keep baking it with the lid on for 10 minutes. Take the lid off, drop the temperature again to 450°F (232°C) and finish baking it for 15 to 20 minutes, or until your loaf is a dark brown.

Remove the bread from the oven, place it on a wire rack and allow it to cool for at least 30 minutes to 1 hour before slicing into it.

sourdough italian

The most common interpretation of a classic Italian bread would be a basic white loaf with an overall soft texture. Generally leavened with commercial yeast for a short and quick rise, these breads' main characteristics are a light thin crust and a dense white crumb. This recipe is a play on a classic Italian loaf but made with sourdough starter to add flavor and complexity. I don't extend fermentation in this bread to avoid developing too much acidity and to maintain a more delicate flavor and I proof and bake the loaves the same day directly in the oven with a small amount of steam to preserve the classic thin crust. To elevate this bread into the perfect sandwich loaf, I use high-protein wheat flour mixed with all-purpose flour. The lower protein content in all-purpose flour balances the overall texture, maintaining the softness typical of an Italian loaf.

yield: 2 loaves

levain

50 g (1.76 oz) high-protein wheat flour

50 g (1.76 oz) water

50 g (1.76 oz) mature starter

final mix

470 g (16.58 oz) high-protein wheat flour

200 g (7.05 oz) all-purpose flour

450 g (15.87 oz) water

150 g (5.29 oz) levain

15 g (0.53 oz) fine sea salt

Start by building the levain 3 to 4 hours before mixing. For more details on my sourdough method, see page 21.

For the final mix, during the last 60 minutes of the levain's fermentation, start the autolyse. In the bowl of a stand mixer fitted with the paddle attachment, combine the high-protein wheat flour, all-purpose flour and water until the flour is fully hydrated and there are no dry bits left. This should take no more than 2 minutes. Cover the bowl with a towel and let it sit at room temperature until the levain reaches peak.

Add your mature levain into the autolysed dough and, using a stand mixer fitted with the dough hook attachment, mix on low (speed 2) for 3 minutes. Increase the speed to medium-high (speed 5) and keep mixing for 5 to 8 minutes, or until the dough has gained strength and is smooth and elastic. Reduce the speed back to low (speed 2) and add the salt. Let it incorporate for 2 minutes, then turn the mixer off, cover the bowl with a towel and let the dough rest for 15 minutes in the machine before taking it out.

Place your dough into a proofing box and start the bulk proof at a temperature between 75°F and 80°F (23°C and 26°C) for 4 hours, performing three sets of coil folds, once every hour.

Transfer the dough onto a lightly floured surface, divide it in two and preshape it by giving each half a round shape, rolling with the help of a dough scraper to tighten the ball. Cover it with a towel and let it rest for 45 minutes at room temperature or in a proofing chamber.

Flip the preshaped dough top side down onto a lightly floured surface and proceed with shaping a simple loaf (page 29). Transfer the loaves onto a sheet tray lined with parchment paper, seam side down, and proof them at room temperature, covered with a towel, for 2 to 3 hours before baking.

Place a deep metal pan filled with lava rocks at the bottom of the oven and preheat it to 500°F (260°C), setting a pizza stone on the lower rack. Score and slide the loaves with the parchment paper onto the preheated pizza stone. Pour a half pint (240 ml) of water onto the lava rocks to create steam and quickly shut the oven. Immediately lower the temperature to 440°F (226°C) and bake it for 15 minutes, then release the steam in the chamber by opening the door just a few inches for 10 to 15 seconds. Lower the temperature again to 420°F (215°C) and keep baking for 10 to 15 minutes, or until golden brown.

Remove the bread from the oven, place it on a wire rack and allow it to cool for at least 30 minutes to 1 hour before slicing into it.

country loaf

This is the artisan sourdough in its purest form, and a great place to start if you're just beginning to bake bread. This loaf utilizes a classic and basic formula that I tried and failed many times when I first started baking. I found that perfecting this loaf helped me immensely to understand the interaction between the four simple ingredients that give birth to this amazing bread. There is no one right way to make this loaf. When comparing the country loaf of different bakers, you can highlight and appreciate their unique style due to the simplicity of the formula. What I love about this recipe is that it allows you to substitute different types of flour, and by experimenting with various grains, you have an opportunity to create your own unique signature loaf.

yield: 2 loaves

825 g (29.1 oz) high-protein wheat flour

600 g (21.16 oz) water

150 g (5.29 oz) mature starter

20 g (0.71 oz) salt

Feed your starter with equal parts water and flour 3 to 4 hours before mixing. For more details on my sourdough method, see page 21.

During the last 60 minutes of your starter's fermentation, start the autolyse. In the bowl of a stand mixer fitted with the paddle attachment, combine the high-protein wheat flour and water until the flour is fully hydrated and there are no dry bits left. This should take no more than 2 minutes. Cover the bowl with a towel or plastic wrap and let the mixture sit at room temperature until the starter reaches peak.

Add your mature starter to the autolysed dough and, using a stand mixer fitted with the dough hook attachment, mix on low (speed 2) for 3 minutes. Increase the speed to medium-high (speed 5) and keep mixing for 5 to 8 minutes, or until the dough has gained strength and is smooth and elastic. Reduce the speed back to low (speed 2) and add the salt. Let it incorporate for 2 minutes, then turn the mixer off, cover the bowl with a towel and let the dough rest for 15 minutes in the machine before taking it out.

Place your dough into a proofing box and start the bulk proof at a temperature between 75°F and 80°F (23°C and 26°C) for 4 hours, performing three sets of coil folds, once every hour.

Transfer your dough onto a lightly floured surface, divide it in two and preshape it by giving each half a round shape, rolling with the help of a dough scraper to tighten the ball. Cover it with a towel and let it rest for 45 minutes at room temperature or in a proofing chamber.

Flip the preshaped dough top side down onto a lightly floured surface, where your dough will relax into a round shape and proceed with shaping the batard (page 29).

Dust two 10-inch (25-cm) oval bannetons with flour and transfer each loaf into the basket, seam side up, then cover with a towel and place in the refrigerator for a final cold proof at 39°F (4°C) for 12 to 16 hours.

Preheat your Dutch oven to 500°F (260°C), line it with a piece of parchment paper and place the proofed loaf in the Dutch oven. Score and bake the loaf with the lid on at 500°F (260°C) for 5 minutes, then drop the temperature to 480°F (248°C) and keep baking with the lid on for 10 minutes. Take the lid off, drop the temperature again to 450°F (232°C) and finish baking for 15 to 20 minutes, or until dark brown.

Remove the bread from the oven, place it on a wire rack and allow it to cool for at least 30 minutes to 1 hour before slicing into it.

whole grain ciabatta

Typically made entirely with white flour, the characteristics of this bread are a very open and airy crumb with a thin and crunchy crust. I'm a big fan of using a percentage of whole grains in my breads, which add not only nutritional value but also flavor and texture, elevating the overall result of the bake. I opted to use red fife whole wheat for the unique flavor and high water absorption of this grain, which allows me to take the hydration of this bread up to 90% and beyond. The result is a perfectly balanced crunchy crust and a soft chewy open crumb that preserves a dark caramelized color with notes of herbs and spices. The versatility of this dough is what makes it one of my favorites to work with. You can shape it into loaves or single rolls for the perfect sandwich bread.

yield: 2 loaves

poolish

250 g (8.82 oz) high-protein wheat flour

250 g (8.82 oz) water

1 g (0.035 oz) baker's yeast

final mix

250 g (8.82 oz) red fife flour

250 g (8.82 oz) high-protein wheat flour

400 g (14.11 oz) water, divided

100 g (3.53 oz) mature starter

15 g (0.53 oz) salt

Start by mixing the poolish the day before. Early in the evening, combine the high-protein wheat flour, water and baker's yeast in a bowl and mix it with a spoon or by hand until all the flour is fully hydrated and there are no dry bits left. Transfer the mixture into a plastic container or leave it in the bowl and proof it for 3 hours, preferably at a temperature between 75°F and 80°F (23°C and 26°C), as indicated in the bulk proof method (page 22), covered with a lid or wrapped in plastic. After proofing at room temperature, place the poolish in the refrigerator, always covered with a towel or plastic wrap, to ferment overnight.

The next morning, feed your starter with equal parts water and flour 3 to 4 hours before mixing. For more details on my sourdough method, see page 21.

For the final mix, during the last 60 minutes of your starter's fermentation, begin the autolyse. In the bowl of a stand mixer fitted with the paddle attachment, combine the red fife flour and high-protein wheat flour with 320 grams (11.29 oz) of the water until the flour is fully hydrated and there are no dry bits left. This should take no more than 2 minutes. Reserve the remaining 80 grams (2.82 oz) of water. Cover the bowl with a towel or plastic wrap and let the mixture sit at room temperature for 1 hour.

Add your mature starter and the poolish to the autolysed dough and, using a stand mixer fitted with the dough hook attachment, mix on low (speed 2) for 3 minutes. Increase the speed to medium-high (speed 5) and keep mixing for 5 to 8 minutes, adding the remaining water slowly in small increments, waiting until the dough absorbs it gradually before adding more. Once all the water is incorporated, reduce the speed back to low (speed 2) and add the salt. Let it incorporate for 2 minutes, then turn the mixer off, cover the bowl with a towel and let the dough rest for 15 minutes in the machine before taking it out. Constantly monitor the temperature of your dough, making sure it doesn't exceed 78°F to 80°F (25°C to 26°C).

Once your dough has rested in the mixing bowl for 15 minutes, transfer it into a shallow rectangular proofing box—this will facilitate shaping the loaves as the dough will relax into a rectangular shape. Bulk proof the dough for 3 hours, as indicated in the bulk proof method (page 22), at a temperature between 75°F and 80°F (24°C and 26°C), performing three sets of coil folds, once every 45 minutes.

(continued)

whole grain ciabatta (continued)

Preheat your oven to 500°F (260°C) and place a deep metal pan filled with lava rocks at the bottom of the oven.

After the bulk proof, flip the proofing box over a generously floured surface and let the dough fall from the container. The dough should have a rectangular shape and feel soft and airy. If you have proofed your dough in a bowl, gently stretch it into a rectangle.

Drape a large kitchen towel or a baguette cloth (couche) onto a large sheet tray, dust it generously with flour and proceed with cutting your ciabatta loaves. With the help of a bench knife or a sharp kitchen knife, divide the dough in half lengthwise into two elongated rectangles and dust the top generously with flour.

Line an 18 x 12–inch (45 x 30–cm) sheet tray with parchment paper and gently transfer the loaves onto the sheet pan. Cover them with a towel and let them rest at room temperature for 30 minutes.

Place the tray with the proofed ciabatta loaves into the oven and pour a half pint (240 ml) of water onto the lava rocks to create steam in the chamber as indicated in the baking method. This will improve the crust development as the steam created keeps the surface of the bread moist in the first stages of baking.

Immediately drop the temperature to 480°F (248°C) and bake your ciabatta for 15 minutes. Release the steam in the chamber by opening the oven door just a few inches for 5 to 10 seconds. Drop the temperature again to 450°F (232°C) and keep baking your ciabatta for 10 to 15 minutes, or until dark golden brown.

Remove the bread from the oven, place it on a wire rack and allow it to cool for at least 30 minutes to 1 hour before slicing into it.

multigrain seeded

This recipe combines different grains, allowing you to achieve the earthy and nutritious bread I always strive for when baking a multigrain bread. I usually add a blend of seeds and grains that in this recipe I make with fifteen different types. The seeds are presoaked and combined into the dough as well as used raw for coating to create an extra crunchy and flavorful crust. Soaking your seed mix before adding it to your dough is an essential step because it hydrates the seeds. This, in turn means that during the long rise they won't absorb moisture from the dough, which would alter its structure. Presoaking your seeds also softens them, making them easier to digest. You may adopt this exact formula or experiment by substituting your favorite blend of seeds. To create an extra layer of flavor, try presoaking your seeds in beer, apple cider or similar flavors.

yield: 2 loaves

levain

80 g (2.82 oz) high-protein wheat flour

80 g (2.82 oz) water

40 g (1.41 oz) mature starter

final mix

130 g (4.59 oz) all-purpose flour

650 g (22.93 oz) high-protein wheat flour

100 g (3.53 oz) whole wheat flour

20 g (0.71 oz) spelt flour

600 g (21.16 oz) water

200 g (7.05 oz) levain

25 g (0.88 oz) fine sea salt

150 g (5.29 oz) presoaked seed mix

Dry seed mix, for coating

seed mix

85 g (3 oz) of each

Rolled oats

Millet

Crushed buckwheat

Sunflower seeds

Pumpkin seeds

50 g (1.76 oz) of each

Red quinoa

White quinoa

Flax seeds

Black sesame

White sesame

Poppy seeds

Amaranth

35 g (1.23 oz) of each

Caraway seeds

Cumin seeds

Fennel seeds

(continued)

Start by building the levain 6 to 8 hours before mixing. For more details on my sourdough method, see page 21.

For the final mix, during the last 60 minutes of the levain's fermentation, start the autolyse. In the bowl of a stand mixer fitted with the paddle attachment, combine the all-purpose flour, high-protein wheat flour, whole wheat flour, spelt flour and water until the flour is fully hydrated and there are no dry bits left. This should take no more than 2 minutes. Cover the bowl with a towel or plastic wrap and let the mixture sit at room temperature until the levain reaches peak.

Add your mature levain to the autolysed dough and, using a stand mixer fitted with the dough hook attachment, mix on low (speed 2) for 3 minutes. Increase the speed to medium-high (speed 5) and keep mixing for 5 to 8 minutes, or until the dough has gained strength and is smooth and elastic. Reduce the speed back to low (speed 2) and add the fine sea salt. Let it incorporate for 2 minutes, then turn the mixer off, cover the bowl with a towel and let the dough rest for 15 minutes in the machine before taking it out.

Place your dough into a proofing box and start the bulk proof at a temperature between 75°F and 80°F (23°C and 26°C) for 4 hours, performing three sets of coil folds, once every hour. Add your soaked seed mix by hand when performing the first fold. Proceed folding normally, even if the seeds are not evenly distributed. They will incorporate evenly by the end of the bulk fermentation after performing the two remaining sets of folds.

Transfer your dough onto a lightly floured surface, divide it in two and preshape it by giving each half a round shape, rolling with the help of a dough scraper to tighten the ball. Cover it with a towel and let it rest for 45 minutes at room temperature or in a proofing chamber.

Line a tray filled with the dry seed mix and proceed with shaping a batard (page 29).

Lightly spray the top of the shaped loaves with water before rolling each one onto the dry seed mix so that the coating will adhere to the surface evenly.

Transfer each loaf into a 10-inch (25-cm) oval banneton, seam side up, cover them with a towel and place them in the refrigerator for a final cold proof at 39°F (4°C) for 12 to 16 hours.

Preheat your Dutch oven to 500°F (260°C), line it with a piece of parchment paper and place the loaf in the Dutch oven. Score and bake the loaf with the lid on at 500°F (260°C) for 10 minutes, then drop the temperature to 450°F (232°C) and keep baking with the lid on for 10 minutes. Take the lid off, drop the temperature again to 430°F (215°C) and finish baking for 15 to 20 minutes, or until dark brown.

Remove the bread from the oven, place it on a wire rack and allow it to cool for at least 30 minutes to 1 hour before slicing into it.

whole grain red fife sourdough

A few years ago my good friend and baker Anthony Ambeliotis (aka the Bread Boss) shared some of his red fife grain with me. Since then I've milled and added a percentage of this incredible grain to many of my creations. Besides its intense flavor, red fife is a grain that allows you to work with high hydration doughs because of the elevated amount of water it absorbs. In this recipe, I autolyse the flour with 80% of the water and, after mixing in the starter and after the gluten has formed, I then add the rest of the water gradually. This allows me to incorporate more water into the dough without compromising the overall structure, resulting in a softer and homogeneous dough with great extensibility. The result is an extremely flavorful and nutritious whole wheat sourdough bread.

yield: 2 loaves

levain

60 g (2.12 oz) high-protein wheat flour

20 g (0.71 oz) red fife flour

80 g (2.82 oz) water

40 g (1.41 oz) mature starter

final mix

500 g (17.64 oz) high-protein wheat flour

400 g (14.11 oz) red fife flour

800 g (28.22 oz) water, divided

200 g (7.05 oz) levain

20 g (0.71 oz) salt

Start by building the levain 6 to 8 hours before mixing. For more details on my sourdough method, see page 21.

For the final mix, during the last 60 minutes of your levain fermentation, start the autolyse. In the bowl of a stand mixer fitted with the paddle attachment, combine the high-protein wheat flour and red fife flour with 700 grams (24.69 oz) of the water until the flour is fully hydrated and there are no dry bits left. This should take no more than 2 minutes. Reserve the rest of the water. Cover the bowl with a towel or plastic wrap and let the mixture sit at room temperature until the levain reaches peak.

Add your mature levain to the autolysed dough and, using a stand mixer fitted with the dough hook attachment, mix on low (speed 2) for 3 minutes. Increase the speed to medium-high (speed 5) and keep mixing for 5 to 8 minutes, adding the remaining 100 grams (3.53 oz) of water slowly in 2 or 3 increments, waiting until the dough absorbs it gradually before adding more. The dough should gain strength and look smooth and elastic. Reduce the speed back to low (speed 2) and add the salt. Let it incorporate for 2 minutes, then turn the mixer off, cover the bowl with a towel and let the dough rest for 15 minutes in the machine before taking it out.

Place your dough into a proofing box and start the bulk proof at a temperature between 75°F and 80°F (23°C and 26°C) for 4 hours, performing three sets of coil folds, once every hour.

Transfer your dough onto a lightly floured surface, divide it in two and preshape it by giving each half a round shape, rolling with the help of a dough scraper to tighten the ball. Cover it with a towel and let it rest for 45 minutes at room temperature or in a proofing chamber.

Flip the preshaped dough top side down on a lightly floured surface. Your dough will relax into a round shape. Proceed with shaping the batard (page 29). Dust two 10-inch (25-cm) oval bannetons with flour and transfer each loaf into the basket, seam side up, then cover them with a towel and place them in the refrigerator for a final cold proof at 39°F (3.9°C) for 12 to 16 hours.

Preheat your Dutch oven to 500°F (260°C), line it with a piece of parchment paper and place the proofed loaf into the Dutch oven. Score and bake the loaf with the lid on at 500°F (260°C) for 5 minutes, drop the temperature to 480°F (248°C) and keep baking with the lid on for 10 minutes. Take the lid off, drop the temperature to 450°F (232°C) and finish baking for 15 to 20 minutes, or until dark brown.

Remove the bread from the oven, place it on a wire rack and allow it to cool for at least 30 minutes to 1 hour before slicing into it.

einkorn baguette

Einkorn is among my favorite grains to work with, and one of the most flavorful. I usually source whole wheat berries and mill them as needed to preserve the unique characteristics and aromas of the grain. Though it has a high protein content, einkorn wheat develops a delicate and silky structure that makes this grain not very suitable to work with when used in high hydration doughs. For that reason, I wanted to develop a hybrid formula that combines sourdough and poolish for a delicious baguette that is both fun to handle and exceptionally flavorful. I found that by prefermenting a good portion of the flour I was able to drastically increase the dough strength and improve the overall texture. The result is a baguette with an extremely moist and aromatic crumb that develops a thin and crunchy crust.

yield: 6 mini baguettes

poolish

200 g (7.05 oz) high-protein wheat flour

200 g (7.05 oz) water

1 g (0.035 oz) baker's yeast

final mix

340 g (11.99 oz) einkorn flour

380 g (13.4 oz) high-protein wheat flour

400 g (14.11 oz) water

160 g (5.64 oz) mature starter

400 g (14.11 oz) poolish

25 g (0.88 oz) salt

Start by mixing the poolish the day before. Early in the afternoon, combine the high-protein wheat flour, water and baker's yeast in a bowl and mix it with a spoon or by hand until all the flour is fully hydrated and there are no dry bits left. Transfer the mixture to a plastic container or leave it in the bowl and proof it for 3 hours, preferably at a temperature between 75°F and 80°F (23°C and 26°C), covered with a lid or wrapped in plastic. After proofing at room temperature, place the poolish in the refrigerator to ferment overnight for 12 hours.

The next day, proceed by feeding your starter with equal parts water and flour 3 to 4 hours before mixing. For more details on my sourdough method, see page 21.

For the final mix, during the last 60 minutes of your starter fermentation, begin the autolyse. In the bowl of a stand mixer fitted with the paddle attachment, combine the einkorn flour, high-protein wheat flour and water until the flour is fully hydrated and there are no dry bits left. This should take no more than 2 minutes. Cover the bowl with a towel or plastic wrap and let the mixture sit at room temperature for 1 hour, or until the sourdough starter reaches peak.

Add your mature starter and the poolish to the autolysed dough and, using a stand mixer fitted with the dough hook attachment, mix on low (speed 2) for 3 minutes. Increase the speed to medium-high (speed 5) and keep mixing for 5 to 8 minutes, or until the dough has gained strength and is smooth and elastic. Reduce the speed back to low (speed 2) and add the salt. Let it incorporate for 3 minutes, then turn the mixer off, cover the bowl with a towel and let the dough rest for 15 minutes in the mixer before taking it out.

Place the dough into a proofing box and bulk proof it for 2 hours, performing four sets of coil folds, once every 30 minutes.

Transfer your dough onto a lightly floured surface, divide it into six equal pieces and preshape it by gently rolling each piece into a rectangular shape. Cover it with a towel and let it rest for 30 minutes at room temperature.

Drape a large kitchen towel or a baguette cloth (couche) onto a large sheet tray, dust it generously with flour and proceed with shaping your baguettes.

(continued)

Working with one piece of dough at a time, transfer the rectangle onto a lightly floured surface and gently flatten it with your hands. Fold the top side toward you over the center of the rectangle, then seal it by pressing with the heel of your hand over the whole length of the folded side. Spin the dough 180 degrees and repeat with the opposite side. Pull and fold the dough to meet the opposite folded side in the center. Press and seal again, then fold the top over the bottom and seal it with the heel of your hand, leaving the seam underneath. Gently roll the shaped dough into an elongated loaf starting from the center and moving outward, applying more pressure as you get to the ends.

After you have shaped them, place each baguette seam side down onto the floured cloth and pull some of the cloth against and between them to create an edge that will function as both support and as a divider between each shaped loaf. Cover them with a towel and proof them for 45 minutes at room temperature—preferably between 75°F and 80°F (24°C and 26°C)—then transfer the shaped baguettes, covered with a towel, into the refrigerator for 1 hour before baking.

Preheat your oven to 500°F (260°C) and place a deep metal pan filled with lava rocks in the bottom of the oven. Set a pizza stone on the lower rack where you will load your baguettes.

Pull the cloth flat onto your counter to space the baguettes and score and flip each loaf onto a baguette flipping board by pulling and lifting the cloth so that the baguette rolls onto the board scored side down. Flip each baguette onto the preheated pizza stone, spacing each loaf at least 2 inches (5 cm) from each other. Try to work relatively quickly as you don't want to lose heat from your oven.

Pour a half pint (240 ml) of water onto the lava rocks to create steam and quickly shut the oven. Immediately lower the oven temperature to 470°F (243°C) and bake the baguettes for 10 minutes, then release the steam in the chamber by opening the door just a few inches for 10 to 15 seconds. Lower the temperature to 450°F (232°C) and finish baking for 10 to 15 minutes, or until golden brown.

Remove the bread from the oven, place it on a wire rack and allow it to cool for at least 30 minutes to 1 hour before slicing into it.

shaping a baguette

After gently flattening the dough into a rectangular shape, fold the bottom side over the center.

Repeat with the opposite side and seal with your thumb along the center line.

Fold the top side over the bottom and, using the palm of your hand, press down to seal the two halves together to create a seam.

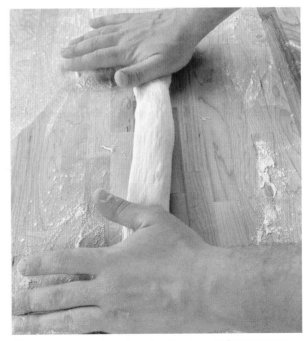

With the seam left underneath, gently roll the baguette from the center outward to elongate the dough.

classic and ancient grains

spelt boule

This ancient grain has a very distinctive flavor and is among my favorites to work with. The high protein content in spelt adds structure and extensibility to the dough, which allows you to easily develop a tender and open crumb. I often find myself adding a percentage of spelt wheat to many of my bakes, even as low as 5%, to enhance the unique flavor and allow this ancient grain to transform my breads. In this recipe, I'm using 20% total spelt flour, which I find to be a perfect amount to create a dough that is easy to work with but that still maintains the flavorful characteristics of this grain. I also add a small amount of spelt flour to the levain to build character and intensify the flavor profile. The final bake is mildly sweet with nutty notes and a soft, flavorful crumb.

yield: 2 loaves

levain

50 g (1.76 oz) high-protein wheat flour

30 g (1.06 oz) spelt flour

80 g (2.82 oz) water

40 g (1.41 oz) mature starter

final mix

730 g (25.75 oz) high-protein wheat flour

170 g (6 oz) spelt flour

690 g (24.34 oz) water

200 g (7.05 oz) levain

25 g (0.88 oz) fine sea salt

300 g (10.58 oz) spelt flakes, for coating

Start by building the levain 6 to 8 hours before mixing. For more details on my sourdough method, see page 21.

For the final mix, during the last 60 minutes of the levain's fermentation, start the autolyse. In the bowl of a stand mixer fitted with the paddle attachment, combine the high-protein wheat flour, spelt flour and water until the flour is fully hydrated and there are no dry bits left. This should take no more than 2 minutes. Cover the bowl with a towel or plastic wrap and let the mixture sit at room temperature until the levain reaches peak.

Add your mature levain to the autolysed dough and, using a stand mixer fitted with the dough hook attachment, mix on low (speed 2) for 3 minutes. Increase the speed to medium-high (speed 5) and keep mixing for 5 to 8 minutes, or until the dough has gained strength and is smooth and elastic. Reduce the speed back to low (speed 2) and add the fine sea salt. Let it incorporate for 2 minutes, then turn the mixer off, cover the bowl with a towel and let the dough rest for 15 minutes in the machine before taking it out.

Place your dough into a proofing box and start the bulk proof at a temperature between 75°F and 80°F (23°C and 26°C) for 4 hours, performing three sets of coil folds, once every hour.

Transfer your dough onto a lightly floured surface, divide it in two and preshape it by giving each half a round shape, rolling with the help of a dough scraper to tighten the ball (page 27). Cover it with a towel and let it rest for 45 minutes at room temperature or in a proofing chamber.

Flip the preshaped dough top side down on a lightly floured surface, where your dough will relax into a round. Line a shallow tray filled with spelt flakes and proceed with shaping the boule (page 29). Lightly spray the top of the shaped loaves with water before rolling each one onto the spelt flakes so that the coating will adhere to the surface evenly. Transfer each loaf into a 10-inch (25-cm) round banneton, flakes side down, and place them into the refrigerator for a cold proof at 39°F (4°C) for 12 to 16 hours.

Preheat your Dutch oven to 500°F (260°C), line it with a piece of parchment paper and place the loaf in the Dutch oven. Bake the loaf with the lid on at 500°F (260°C) for 10 minutes, then drop the temperature to 450°F (232°C) and keep baking with the lid on for 10 minutes. Take the lid off, drop the temperature again to 430°F (215°C) and finish baking for 15 to 20 minutes, or until dark golden brown.

Remove the bread from the oven, place it on a wire rack and allow it to cool for at least 30 minutes to 1 hour before slicing into it.

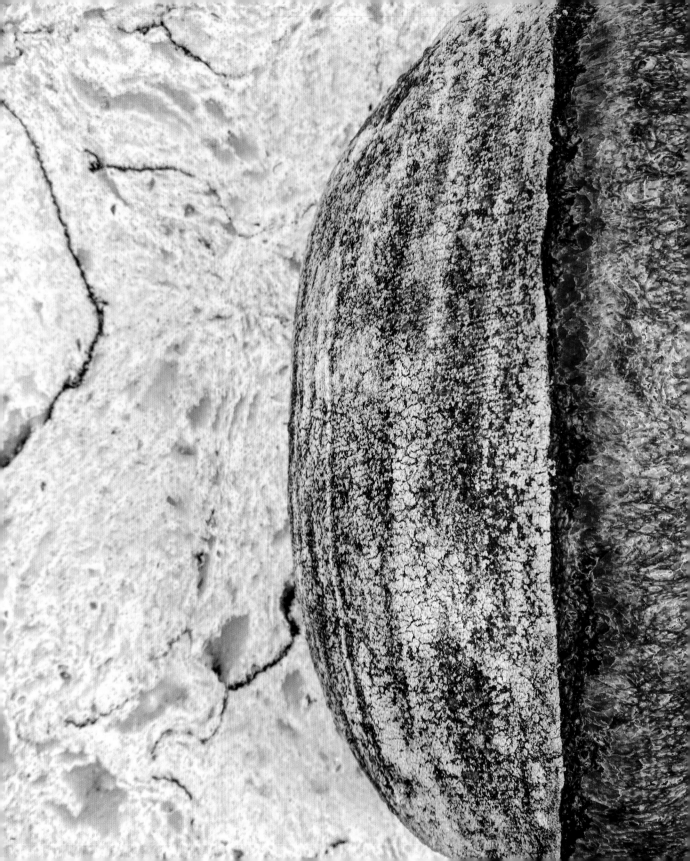

khorasan wheat bread

Compared to other wheat, khorasan develops a dough with a unique smooth texture and transforms the final bake by developing an intense nutty and buttery flavor. This unique grain is able to elevate your bread even when used in small percentages and is a fun one to work with. The high protein content in khorasan wheat allows the dough to absorb a high percentage of water. In this recipe, I wanted to highlight the deep flavor and texture that this grain develops. With that in mind, I used a total of 50% khorasan flour, which gives the bread a golden crust as well as a unique dark brown and extremely moist and chewy crumb.

yield: 2 loaves

levain

50 g (1.76 oz) high-protein wheat flour

30 g (1.06 oz) khorasan flour

80 g (2.82 oz) water

40 g (1.41 oz) mature starter

final mix

430 g (15.17 oz) high-protein wheat flour

470 g (16.58 oz) khorasan flour

690 g (24.34 oz) water

200 g (7.05 oz) levain

25 g (0.88 oz) fine sea salt

Start by building the levain 6 to 8 hours before mixing. For more details on my sourdough method, see page 21.

For the final mix, during the last 60 minutes of the levain's fermentation, start the autolyse. In the bowl of a stand mixer fitted with the paddle attachment, combine the high-protein wheat flour, khorasan flour and water until the flour is fully hydrated and there are no dry bits left. This should take no more than 2 minutes. Cover the bowl with a towel or plastic wrap and let the mixture sit at room temperature until the levain reaches peak.

Add your mature levain to the autolysed dough and, using a stand mixer fitted with the dough hook attachment, mix on low (speed 2) for 3 minutes. Increase the speed to medium-high (speed 5) and keep mixing for 5 to 8 minutes, or until the dough has gained strength and is smooth and elastic. Reduce the speed back to low (speed 2) and add the fine sea salt. Let it incorporate for 2 minutes, then turn the mixer off, cover the bowl with a towel and let the dough rest for 15 minutes in the machine before taking it out.

Place your dough into a proofing box and start the bulk proof at a temperature between 75°F and 80°F (23°C and 26°C) for 4 hours, performing three sets of coil folds, once every hour.

Transfer your dough onto a lightly floured surface, divide it in two and preshape it by giving each half a round shape, rolling with the help of a dough scraper to tighten the ball. Cover it with a towel and let it rest for 45 minutes at room temperature or in a proofing chamber.

Flip the preshaped dough top side down on a lightly floured surface, where your dough will relax into a round. Proceed with shaping the batard (page 29).

Transfer each loaf into a 10-inch (25-cm) oval banneton dusted with khorasan flour, seam side up, and place them in the refrigerator for a cold proof at 39°F (4°C) for 12 to 16 hours.

Preheat your Dutch oven to 500°F (260°C), line it with a cut-out piece of parchment paper and place the loaf in the Dutch oven. Score and bake the loaf with the lid on at 500°F (260°C) for 10 minutes, then drop the temperature to 450°F (232°C) and keep baking with the lid on for 10 minutes. Take the lid off, drop the temperature again to 430°F (215°C) and finish baking for 15 to 20 minutes, or until dark golden brown.

Remove the bread from the oven, place it on a wire rack and allow it to cool for at least 30 minutes to 1 hour before slicing into it.

emmer/farro bread

Farro includes different varieties of wheat, like spelt, emmer and einkorn. It's one the most popular and versatile ancient grains used around the globe and, in my opinion, one of the most delicious to work with when it comes to baking bread and pastries. Emmer particularly makes a wholesome bread when used in high percentages, and is a nutritious and extremely flavorful grain. In this recipe, I wanted to find the perfect balance of emmer, making sure to highlight the acidity of the overall bake and creating an open crumb but still preserving the intense aromas that emmer develops. The result is a nutty and earthy loaf with an amazingly chewy crumb and an extra crunchy crust thanks to the cracked emmer wheat coating the top that adds a layer of texture and flavor.

yield: 2 loaves

levain

50 g (1.76 oz) high-protein wheat flour

30 g (1.06 oz) emmer flour

80 g (2.82 oz) water

40 g (1.41 oz) mature starter

final mix

700 g (24.69 oz) high-protein wheat flour

200 g (7.05 oz) emmer flour

680 g (23.99 oz) water

200 g (7.05 oz) levain

20 g (0.71 oz) salt

Cracked emmer wheat, for coating

Start by building the levain 6 to 8 hours before mixing. For more details on my sourdough method, see page 21.

For the final mix, during the last 60 minutes of your levain fermentation, start the autolyse. In the bowl of a stand mixer fitted with the paddle attachment, combine the high-protein wheat flour, emmer flour and water until the flour is fully hydrated and there are no dry bits. This should take no more than 2 minutes. Cover the bowl with a towel and let the mixture sit at room temperature until the levain reaches peak.

Add your mature levain to the autolysed dough and, using a stand mixer fitted with the dough hook attachment, mix on low (speed 2) for 3 minutes. Increase the speed to medium-high (speed 5) and keep mixing for 5 to 8 minutes, or until the dough has gained strength and is smooth and elastic. Reduce the speed back to low (speed 2) and add the salt. Let it incorporate for 2 minutes, then turn the mixer off, cover the bowl with a towel and let the dough rest for 15 minutes before taking it out.

Place your dough into a proofing box and start the bulk proof at a temperature between 75°F and 80°F (23°C and 26°C) for 4 hours, performing three sets of coil folds, once every hour.

Transfer your dough onto a lightly floured surface, divide it in two and preshape it by giving each half a round shape, rolling with the help of a dough scraper to tighten the ball. Cover it with a towel and let it rest for 45 minutes at room temperature or in a proofing chamber.

Flip the preshaped dough top side down onto a lightly floured surface, where your dough will relax into a round. Proceed with shaping the batard (page 29). Lightly spray the top of the shaped loaves with water before rolling each one onto the cracked emmer wheat so that the coating will adhere to the surface evenly.

Dust two 10-inch (25-cm) oval bannetons with flour and transfer each loaf into the basket, seam side up, then cover them with a towel and place them in the refrigerator for a final cold proof at 39°F (4°C) for 12 to 16 hours.

Preheat your Dutch oven to 500°F (260°C), line it with a piece of parchment paper and place the proofed loaf in the Dutch oven. Score and bake the loaf with the lid on at 500°F (260°C) for 5 minutes, then drop the temperature to 480°F (248°C) and keep baking with the lid on for 10 minutes. Take the lid off, drop the temperature again to 450°F (232°C) and finish baking for 15 to 20 minutes, or until dark brown.

Remove the bread from the oven, place it on a wire rack and allow it to cool for at least 30 minutes to 1 hour before slicing into it.

Specialty Breads

This chapter is meant to be playful and whimsical. Here I want to showcase more advanced and unique recipes, so I recommend you make sure that you are comfortable baking the classic breads in the previous chapter (page 33) first before trying these more adventurous recipes. As a trained chef, I love to experiment with color, flavor and texture when conceptualizing a dining experience. In the following chapter, I'll share with you some of the techniques I have found to be complementary in the art of baking bread. These loaves are unexpected. You'll surprise your loved ones or dinner guests with something they have never tried before. In this chapter, I want to express my creativity by infusing into these loaves years of traveling and exploring ingredients and techniques. From the flavor and texture in the Spanish Sourdough (page 74) to the vibrant visual of the Sourdough Morado (page 69), the following recipes will take you on a journey that will stimulate all of your senses.

purple sweet potato bread

To me, this is one of the most stunning and photogenic breads. By steaming and incorporating the sweet potato into the dough, you'll be able to preserve a subtle flavor and a vibrant purple shade. I wanted to naturally create a bright color contrast between the two laminated doughs. This result is achieved by making two distinct doughs that are proofed separately and then combined at the end of the bulk proof. By laminating and incorporating the two doughs at the end stages of fermentation, you'll be able to maintain a dichotomy between the two colors. If the doughs were to be combined at the beginning stages of fermentation, the two colors would meld into a denser color pattern, losing the distinct bright contrast. The result is a surprising and visually vibrant loaf with all the familiar characteristics of a flavorful sourdough bread.

yield: 2 loaves

sweet potato dough

220 g (7.76 oz) purple sweet potato

450 g (15.87 oz) high-protein wheat flour

340 g (11.99 oz) water

90 g (3.17 oz) mature starter

10 g (0.35 oz) salt

white sourdough

450 g (15.87 oz) high-protein wheat flour

340 g (11.99 oz) water

100 g (3.53 oz) mature starter

10 g (0.35 oz) salt

Start by feeding your starter with equal parts water and flour 3 to 4 hours before mixing. For more details on my sourdough method, see page 21.

For the sweet potato dough, prepare your steamed potatoes. Place a steamer basket or a colander in a large pot. Add water until it reaches 1 or 2 inches (2.5 or 5 cm) below the bottom of the basket. Put the sweet potatoes in the basket and bring the water to a boil. Once the water is boiling, cover the pot, reduce the heat to medium and allow the potatoes to steam until you can insert a paring knife without resistance, 30 minutes. Using tongs, remove the potatoes from the steamer basket and let them rest for 5 minutes. Peel the potatoes while hot using a clean towel and a paring knife, cover them loosely with plastic wrap and place them in the refrigerator to cool completely.

During the last 60 minutes of your sourdough starter fermentation, begin the autolyse on both doughs.

Starting with the sweet potato dough, in the bowl of a stand mixer fitted with the paddle attachment, combine the high-protein wheat flour and water until the flour is fully hydrated and there are no dry bits left. This should take no more than 2 minutes. Transfer the mixture to a bowl, cover it with plastic wrap and set it aside.

Repeat the process with the white sourdough. Cover the bowl with plastic wrap and let the mixture sit at room temperature to autolyse until the starter reaches peak.

Begin by mixing the sweet potato dough. Incorporate 90 grams (3.17 oz) of your mature starter and the cooled steamed potatoes into the autolysed dough and, using a stand mixer fitted with the dough hook attachment, mix on low (speed 2) for 3 minutes. Increase the speed to medium-high (speed 5) and keep mixing for 5 to 8 minutes, or until the dough has gained strength and is smooth and elastic. Reduce the speed back to low (speed 2) and add the salt. Let it incorporate for 2 minutes, then turn the mixer off, cover the bowl with a towel and let the dough rest for 15 minutes in the machine before taking it out.

Next, mix the white sourdough. Incorporate 100 grams (3.53 oz) of your mature starter into the autolysed dough and proceed with mixing following the method listed above that you used to mix the sweet potato dough.

(continued)

Place the two doughs into two separate proofing boxes and begin the bulk proof process at a temperature between 75°F and 80°F (23°C and 26°C) for 4 hours, performing three sets of coil folds, once every hour.

One hour after the third set of coil folds, proceed with the lamination process to combine the two doughs (see page 24 for step-by-step photos of the bi-color lamination process). Spray your work surface with abundant water to prevent the dough from sticking. I suggest you avoid laminating on a wood counter surface as the wood will immediately absorb the water and your dough will stick to the surface—a marble or similar smooth countertop is preferred. Working with one dough at a time, transfer the dough onto the sprayed counter and stretch it into a ½- to 1-inch (1.3- to 2.5-cm)-thick rectangle by gently pulling and stretching the edges, making sure not to tear the dough.

Repeat the process and stretch the second dough right next to the first one, making sure they match in size as much as possible.

Pick up the purple dough and lay half of it over half of the white dough, then fold the remaining half of the white dough over the purple dough and do the same for the last purple half.

Now that you have overlapped the four different color layers evenly, pick up and pull the top side of the dough upward and fold it over the center. Repeat this step, folding the dough toward you until the seam is left underneath. Transfer the laminated dough into a proofing box, cover it with plastic wrap and let it rest at a temperature between 75°F and 80°F (23°C and 26°C) for 1 hour before preshaping.

Transfer the dough onto a lightly floured surface, divide it in two and preshape it by giving each half a round shape, rolling with the help of a dough scraper to tighten the ball. Place the preshaped doughs back into separate proofing boxes or two mixing bowls and cover them with a towel or plastic wrap. Let them rest for 45 minutes at room temperature or in a proofing chamber.

Working with one dough at a time, flip the preshaped dough top side down onto a lightly floured surface and proceed with shaping your batards (page 29).

Dust two 10-inch (25-cm) oval bannetons with flour and transfer each loaf into the basket, seam side up, then cover them with a towel and place them in the refrigerator for a final cold proof at 39°F (4°C) for 12 to 16 hours.

Preheat your Dutch oven to 500°F (260°C), line it with a piece of parchment paper and place the proofed loaf in the Dutch oven. Score and bake the loaf with the lid on at 500°F (260°C) for 5 minutes, drop the temperature to 480°F (248°C) and keep baking with the lid on for 10 minutes. Take the lid off, drop the temperature to 450°F (232°C) and finish baking for 15 to 20 minutes, or until dark golden brown.

Remove the bread from the oven, place it on a wire rack and allow it to cool for at least 30 minutes to 1 hour before slicing into it.

spiced marble chocolate sourdough

Cozy up with a slice of this bread. The warmth of the spices combined with the dark chocolate create a loaf that gives you the nostalgia of holiday flavors without being overly sweet. I decided to blend two different color doughs, both including spices, to create a swirl effect, along with the addition of orange zest to the chocolate dough for a subtle citrus note. Coarsely chopped dark chocolate is also incorporated into the loaf during lamination so it can disperse evenly throughout the dough, which will melt into tiny rich pockets when toasted. I mostly bake this as a seasonal loaf in the fall and winter months, though it can be an indulgent treat for any time of year. This rich and aromatic bread can be enjoyed by itself or paired with all kinds of preserves and nut butters.

yield: 2 loaves

spice mix

3 g (0.11 oz) whole cloves

2 g (0.07 oz) whole cardamom

8 g (0.28 oz) whole allspice

10 g (0.35 oz) ground cinnamon

5 g (0.18 oz) freshly grated nutmeg

spiced dough

300 g (10.58 oz) high-protein wheat flour

150 g (5.29 oz) all-purpose flour

340 g (11.99 oz) water

100 g (3.53 oz) mature starter

3 g (0.11 oz) spice mix

10 g (0.35 oz) salt

chocolate dough

300 g (10.58 oz) high-protein wheat flour

150 g (5.29 oz) all-purpose flour

15 g (0.53 oz) dark cocoa powder

340 g (11.99 oz) water

90 g (3.17 oz) mature starter

3 g (0.11 oz) spice mix

Zest of 1 large orange

10 g (0.35 oz) salt

lamination

150 g (5.29 oz) 70% dark chocolate

Start by feeding your starter with equal parts water and flour 3 to 4 hours before mixing. For more details on my sourdough method, see page 21.

Prepare your spice mix by grinding the cloves, cardamom and allspice together, then add the ground cinnamon and freshly grated nutmeg and stir them to combine. Alternatively, source preground spices and mix them together. Store them in an airtight container.

During the last 60 minutes of your sourdough starter fermentation, begin the autolyse on both doughs.

Starting with the spiced dough, in the bowl of a stand mixer fitted with the paddle attachment, combine the high-protein wheat flour, all-purpose flour and water until the flour is fully hydrated and there are no dry bits left. This should take no more than 2 minutes. Transfer the mixture to a bowl, cover it with a towel or plastic wrap and set it aside.

Repeat this process with the chocolate dough, this time mixing all of the high-protein wheat flour, all-purpose flour, dark cocoa powder and water together. Cover the bowl with plastic wrap and let the two doughs autolyse at room temperature until the starter reaches peak.

Proceed with your mixing, starting with the chocolate dough. Add 90 grams (3.17 oz) of your mature starter, the spice mix and the orange zest to the autolysed dough and, using a stand mixer fitted with the dough hook attachment, mix on low (speed 2) for 3 minutes. Increase the speed to medium-high (speed 5) and keep mixing for 5 to 8 minutes, or until the dough has gained strength and is smooth and elastic. Reduce the speed back to low (speed 2) and add the salt. Let it incorporate for 2 minutes, then turn the mixer off, cover the bowl with a towel and let the dough rest for 15 minutes in the machine before taking it out.

Next, mix the spiced dough. Add 100 grams (3.53 oz) of your mature starter and the spice mix to the autolysed dough and proceed following the method listed above that you used for the chocolate dough.

Place the two doughs into two separate proofing boxes and begin the bulk proof fermentation at a temperature between 75°F and 80°F (23°C and 26°C) for 4 hours, performing three sets of coil folds, once every hour.

In the meantime, roughly chop the dark chocolate and set it aside.

(continued)

One hour after the third set of coil folds, proceed with the lamination process to combine the two doughs (see page 24 for step-by-step photos). Spray your work surface with abundant water to prevent the dough from sticking. I suggest you avoid laminating on a wood counter surface as the wood will immediately absorb the water and your dough will stick to the surface—a marble or similar smooth countertop is preferred.

Working with one dough at a time, transfer the dough onto the sprayed counter and stretch it into a ½- to 1-inch (1.3- to 2.5-cm)-thick rectangle by gently pulling and stretching the edges, making sure not to tear the dough.

Repeat the process and stretch the second dough right next to the first one, making sure they match in size as much as possible. Once both doughs are stretched and next to each other, sprinkle the chopped dark chocolate evenly over the surface of both doughs.

Pick up the chocolate dough and lay half of it over half of the white dough, then fold the remaining half of the white dough over the chocolate one and do the same for the last chocolate half.

Now that you overlapped the four different layers evenly, alternating colors with every layer, pick up and pull the top side of the dough upward and fold it over the center. Repeat folding toward you until the seam is left underneath. Transfer the laminated dough into a proofing box, cover it with plastic wrap and let it rest at a temperature between 75°F and 80°F (23°C and 26°C) for 1 hour before preshaping.

Transfer the dough onto a lightly floured surface, divide it in two and preshape it by giving each half a round shape, rolling with the help of a dough scraper to tighten the ball. Place the preshaped doughs back into separate proofing boxes or two mixing bowls and cover them with a towel or plastic wrap. Let them rest for 45 minutes at room temperature or in a proofing chamber.

Working with one dough at a time, flip the preshaped dough top side down onto a lightly floured surface and proceed with shaping your batards (page 29).

Dust two 10-inch (25-cm) oval bannetons with flour and transfer each loaf into the basket, seam side up. Cover them with a towel and place them in the refrigerator for a final cold proof at 39°F (4°C) for 12 to 16 hours.

Preheat your Dutch oven to 500°F (260°C), line it with a piece of parchment paper and place the proofed loaf in the Dutch oven. Score and bake the loaf with the lid on at 500°F (260°C) for 5 minutes, then drop the temperature to 480°F (248°C) and keep baking with the lid on for 10 minutes. Take the lid off, drop the temperature again to 450°F (232°C) and finish baking for 15 to 20 minutes, or until dark brown.

Remove the bread from the oven, place it on a wire rack and allow it to cool for at least 30 minutes to 1 hour before slicing into it.

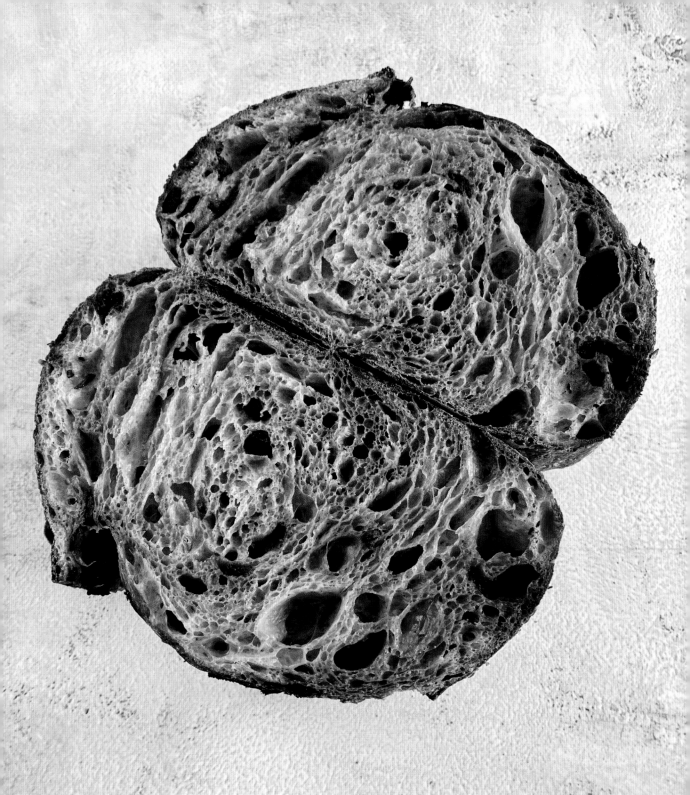

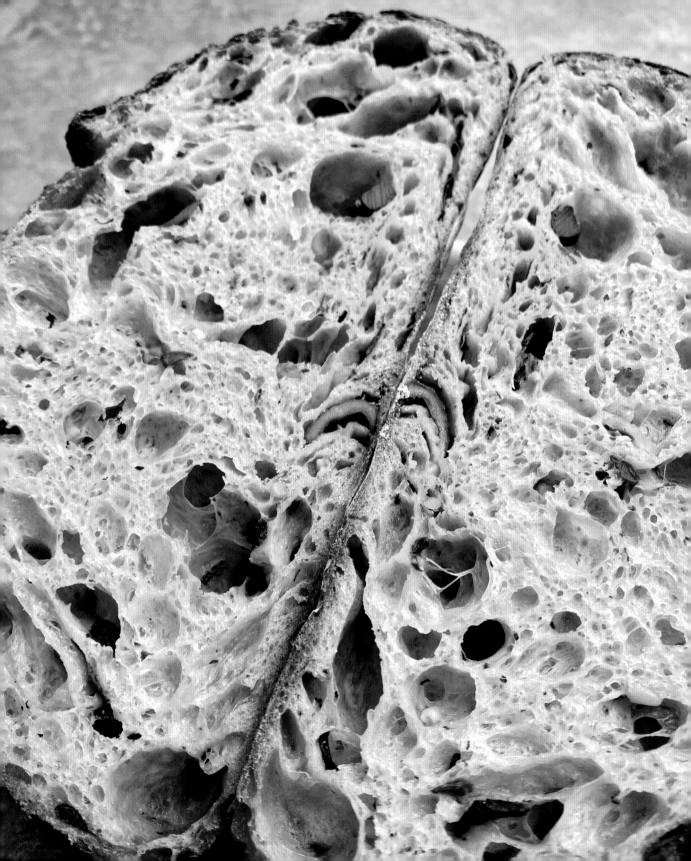

brown butter–mushroom oat–porridge bread

I'm a big fan of savory oat porridge. There really are infinite possibilities when it comes to adding ingredients to a creamy oatmeal, sweet or savory. I'm also a huge fan of using cooked grains in my breads. They add extraordinary texture to the loaf, making the crumb chewier and extremely moist. In this recipe, I wanted to combine the texture of a sourdough loaf with an umami-rich mushroom porridge enriched with browned butter for a nutty and earthy flavor profile. When adding cooked grains to your breads, you want to make sure to cook them thoroughly and to a thick consistency, otherwise they might compromise the overall structure of the dough, even if added in small percentages, as they add moisture and could interfere with the final hydration.

yield: 1 loaf

levain

40 g (1.41 oz) high-protein wheat flour

40 g (1.41 oz) water

20 g (0.71 oz) mature starter

mushroom porridge

200 g (7.05 oz) cremini mushrooms

200 g (7.05 oz) shiitake mushrooms

40 g (1.41 oz) unsalted butter

1 clove garlic, peeled and crushed

10 fresh sage leaves

60 g (2.12 oz) water

40 g (1.41 oz) steel-cut oats

final mix

130 g (4.59 oz) high-protein wheat flour

300 g (10.58 oz) all-purpose flour

20 g (0.71 oz) whole wheat flour

320 g (11.29 oz) water

100 g (3.53 oz) levain

10 g (0.35 oz) salt

100 g (3.53 oz) mushroom porridge

Start by building the levain 6 to 8 hours before mixing. For more details on my sourdough method, see page 21.

Begin preparing the mushroom porridge. Clean your mushrooms by wiping them with a moist paper towel and slicing them to a ¼-inch (6-mm) thickness. Set them aside.

Add the butter to a small saucepan and cook it over medium-low heat for 5 to 8 minutes, or until it browns. Swirl the pan occasionally to be sure the butter is cooking evenly.

In the meantime, line a fine-mesh strainer with a coffee filter or a paper towel and set it over a medium sauté pan.

Once the butter is browned, pour it over the strainer and into the pan to filter out the milk solids. Discard the solids and add the garlic to the pan. Set the pan over low heat and slowly cook the garlic for 5 minutes, making sure the garlic doesn't turn dark brown. Finely chop the sage leaves and add them to the pan. Keep cooking for 1 to 2 minutes, then add the sliced mushrooms. Sauté the mushrooms over medium heat for 10 minutes, stirring often.

While cooking the mushrooms, start preparing the oat porridge. In a medium saucepan, bring the water to a simmer over medium heat, then reduce the heat to low and add the oats. Slowly simmer the oats for 5 minutes, then add the mushrooms to the porridge and keep simmering for 10 to 15 minutes, or until the mixture is thick. Remove the garlic clove and cool the porridge in the refrigerator for 1 to 2 hours.

For the final mix, during the last 60 minutes of the levain's fermentation, start the autolyse. In the bowl of a stand mixer fitted with the paddle attachment, combine the high-protein wheat flour, all-purpose flour, whole wheat flour and water until the flour is fully hydrated and there are no dry bits left. This should take no more than 2 minutes. Cover the bowl with a towel or plastic wrap and let the mixture sit at room temperature until the levain reaches peak.

(continued)

brown–butter mushroom
oat–porridge bread (continued)

Add your mature levain to the autolysed dough and, using a stand mixer fitted with the dough hook attachment, mix on low (speed 2) for 3 minutes. Increase the speed to medium-high (speed 5) and keep mixing for 5 to 8 minutes, or until the dough has gained strength and is smooth and elastic. Reduce the speed back to low (speed 2) and add the salt. Let it incorporate for 2 minutes, then turn the mixer off, cover the bowl with a towel and let the dough rest for 15 minutes in the machine before taking it out.

Place the dough into a proofing box and start the bulk proof at a temperature between 75°F and 80°F (23°C and 26°C) for 4 hours, performing three sets of coil folds, once every hour. Add the cooled porridge to the dough when performing the first coil fold and don't worry if it looks like the porridge is not evenly absorbed right away—it will distribute evenly throughout the bulk fermentation as you keep performing folds.

Transfer your dough onto a lightly floured surface and preshape it, giving it a round shape by rolling with the help of a dough scraper to tighten it into a ball. Cover it with a towel and let it rest for 45 minutes at room temperature or in a proofing chamber.

Flip the dough onto a lightly floured surface and proceed with shaping the batard (page 29).

Dust a 10-inch (25-cm) oval banneton with flour. Transfer the shaped loaf into the basket, top side down, and place it in the refrigerator for a cold proof at 39°F (3.9°C) for 12 to 16 hours.

Preheat your Dutch oven to 500°F (260°C), line it with a piece of parchment paper and place the loaf in the Dutch oven. Bake the loaf with the lid on at 500°F (260°C) for 10 minutes, drop the temperature to 450°F (232°C) and keep baking with the lid on for 10 minutes. Take the lid off, drop the temperature again to 430°F (215°C) and finish baking for 15 to 20 minutes, or until dark golden brown.

Remove the bread from the oven, place it on a wire rack and allow it to cool for at least 30 minutes to 1 hour before slicing into it.

sourdough morado

The inspiration for this loaf comes from my love for Mexican culture. Corn is arguably the grain that forms the foundation of Mexican cuisine. I chose a purple heirloom variety for its intense color and flavor. This is definitely a fun dough to work with. The purple corn flour is soaked in boiling water and left to rehydrate until it transforms into a deep violet paste. When incorporated into the dough, the soaked purple corn flour infuses a vibrant and vivid purple shade and adds a layer of texture to the final baked loaf. The corn flour I used in this recipe is from Mama Tere. Similar to the Purple Sweet Potato Bread (page 61), here I also mixed two different doughs that are fermented separately and combined with lamination. The result is a vibrant and flavorful sourdough with a tender and moist crumb that develops delicate notes of mild sweet corn.

yield: 2 loaves

purple corn dough

420 g (14.82 oz) water, divided

50 g (1.76 oz) purple corn flour

450 g (15.87 oz) high-protein wheat flour

100 g (3.53 oz) mature starter

10 g (0.35 oz) salt

white sourdough

450 g (15.87 oz) high-protein wheat flour

330 g (11.64 oz) water

90 g (3.17 oz) mature starter

10 g (0.35 oz) salt

Start by feeding your starter with equal parts water and flour 3 to 4 hours before mixing. For more details on my sourdough method, see page 21.

For the purple corn dough, begin by soaking the purple corn flour. In a small saucepan, bring 100 grams (3.53 oz) of water to a gentle boil, then remove it from the heat and stir in the purple corn flour. Mix it together with a spoon until all the water is absorbed and there are no dry bits left. Cover the pan with a folded towel and let the mixture cool at room temperature for at least 1 hour.

During the last 60 minutes of your sourdough starter fermentation, begin the autolyse on both doughs.

Starting with the purple corn dough, in the bowl of a stand mixer fitted with the paddle attachment, combine the high-protein wheat flour and 320 grams (11.29 oz) of water until the flour is fully hydrated and there are no dry bits left. This should take no more than 2 minutes. Transfer the mixture to a bowl, cover it with plastic wrap and set it aside.

Repeat the process for the white sourdough. Transfer the mixture to a bowl, cover it with plastic wrap and let the mixture sit at room temperature until the starter reaches peak.

Begin mixing the white sourdough. Add 90 grams (3.17 oz) of your mature starter to the autolysed dough and, using a stand mixer fitted with the dough hook attachment, mix on low (speed 2) for 3 minutes. Increase the speed to medium-high (speed 5) and keep mixing for 5 to 8 minutes, or until the dough has gained strength and is smooth and elastic. Reduce the speed back to low (speed 2) and add the salt. Let it incorporate for 2 minutes, then turn the mixer off, cover the bowl with a towel and let the dough rest for 15 minutes in the machine before taking it out.

Proceed with mixing the purple corn dough. Incorporate 100 grams (3.53 oz) of starter and the blue corn mixture into the autolysed dough and proceed with your mixing following the method listed above that you used to mix the white sourdough.

Place the two doughs into two separate proofing boxes and begin the bulk proof at a temperature between 75°F and 80°F (23°C and 26°C) for 4 hours, performing three sets of coil folds, once every hour.

One hour after the third set of coil folds, proceed with the lamination process to combine the two doughs (see page 24 for step-by-step photos of the bi-color lamination process). Spray your work surface with abundant water to prevent the dough from sticking. I suggest you avoid laminating on a wood counter surface as the wood will immediately absorb the water and your dough will stick to the surface—a marble or similar smooth countertop is preferred. Working with one dough at a time, transfer the dough onto the sprayed counter and stretch it into a ½- to 1-inch (1.3- to 2.5-cm)-thick rectangle by pulling and stretching the edges gently, making sure not to tear the dough.

Repeat the process and stretch the second dough right next to the first one, making sure they match in size as much as possible. Once both doughs are stretched next to each other, pick up the purple dough and lay half of it over half of the white dough, then fold the remaining half of the white dough over the purple dough and do the same for the last purple half.

Now that you have overlapped the four different color layers evenly, pick up and pull the top side of the dough upward and fold it over the center. Repeat this process, rolling the dough toward you until the seam is left underneath. Transfer the laminated dough back into the proofing box, cover it with plastic wrap and let it rest at a temperature between 75°F and 80°F (23°C and 26°C) for 1 hour before preshaping.

Transfer the dough onto a lightly floured surface, divide it in two and preshape it by giving each half a round shape, rolling with the help of a dough scraper to tighten the ball. Place the preshaped doughs back into separate proofing boxes or two mixing bowls and cover them with a towel or plastic wrap. Let them rest for 45 minutes at room temperature or in a proofing chamber.

Working with one dough at a time, flip the preshaped dough top side down onto a lightly floured surface and proceed with shaping your batards (page 29).

Dust two 10-inch (25-cm) oval bannetons with flour and transfer each loaf into their individual baskets seam side up, then cover them with a towel and place them in the refrigerator for a final cold proof at 39°F (4°C) for 12 to 16 hours.

Preheat your Dutch oven to 500°F (260°C), line it with a piece of parchment paper and place the proofed loaf in the Dutch oven. Score then bake the loaf with the lid on at 500°F (260°C) for 5 minutes. Drop the temperature to 480°F (248°C) and keep baking with the lid on for 10 minutes. Take the lid off, drop the temperature again to 450°F (232°C) and finish baking for 15 to 20 minutes, or until dark brown.

Remove the bread from the oven, place it on a wire rack and allow it to cool for at least 30 minutes to 1 hour before slicing into it.

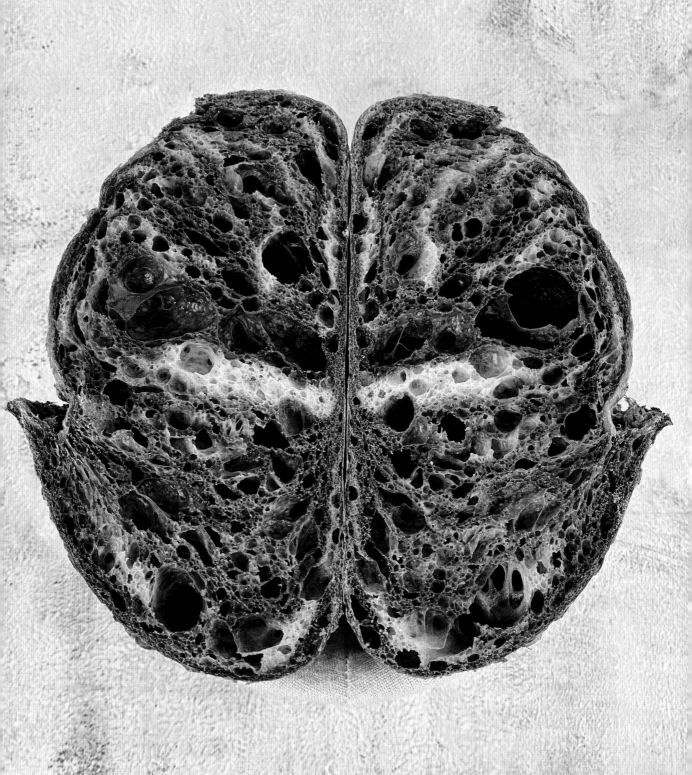

green olive sourdough

When thinking of the bread or focaccia I ate while growing up, I always recall the ones that included some type of olives. The addition of toasted caraway seeds in this recipe balances perfectly with the sweet and tangy flavor of the Castelvetrano olives. Like many of the seed mixes, porridge and other various inclusions, I prefer to incorporate any additional ingredients to my dough when performing folds or with lamination to make sure not to compromise the gluten structure.

yield: 2 loaves

levain
80 g (2.82 oz) high-protein wheat flour

80 g (2.82 oz) water

40 g (1.41 oz) mature starter

final mix
750 g (26.46 oz) high-protein wheat flour

100 g (3.53 oz) all-purpose flour

50 g (1.76 oz) whole wheat flour

700 g (24.69 oz) water

20 g (0.71 oz) caraway seeds

190 g (6.7 oz) pitted Castelvetrano olives

200 g (7.05 oz) levain

20 g (0.71 oz) salt

Start by building the levain 6 to 8 hours before mixing. For more details on my sourdough method, see page 21. For the final mix, during the last 60 minutes of your starter's fermentation, start the autolyse. In the bowl of a stand mixer fitted with the paddle attachment, combine the high-protein wheat flour, all-purpose flour, whole wheat flour and water until the flour is fully hydrated and there are no dry bits left. This should take no more than 2 minutes. Cover the bowl with a towel or plastic wrap and let the mixture sit at room temperature until the starter reaches peak.

Toast the caraway seeds in a dry skillet over medium-high heat for 2 to 3 minutes, or until they are fragrant. Remove them from the pan and let them cool to room temperature. Drain any liquid from your olives and cut them in half. Set them aside.

Add your mature levain to the autolysed dough and, using a stand mixer fitted with the dough hook attachment, mix on low (speed 2) for 3 minutes. Increase the speed to medium-high (speed 5) and keep mixing for 5 to 8 minutes, or until the dough has gained strength and is smooth and elastic. Reduce the speed back to low (speed 2) and add the salt. Let it incorporate for 2 minutes, then turn the mixer off, cover the bowl with a towel and let the dough rest for 15 minutes in the machine before taking it out.

Place your dough into a proofing box and start the bulk proof at a temperature between 75°F and 80°F (23°C and 26°C) for 4 hours, performing three sets of coil folds, once every hour. Sprinkle the olives and caraway seeds over the dough when performing the first coil fold. Don't worry if they fall off into the proofing box or are not evenly absorbed into the dough—they will distribute evenly throughout the bulk fermentation as you keep performing folds.

Transfer your dough onto a lightly floured surface, divide it in two and preshape it, giving each half a round shape, rolling with the help of a dough scraper to tighten the ball. Cover them with a towel and let them rest for 45 minutes to 1 hour at room temperature or in a proofing chamber. Flip the preshaped dough top side down onto a lightly floured surface and proceed with shaping the batards (page 29). Dust two 10-inch (25-cm) oval bannetons with flour and transfer each loaf into the basket, seam side up, then cover them with a towel and place them in the refrigerator for a final cold proof at 39°F (4°C) for 12 to 16 hours.

Preheat your Dutch oven to 500°F (260°C), line it with a piece of parchment paper and place the proofed loaf in the Dutch oven. Score and bake the loaf with the lid on at 500°F (260°C) for 5 minutes, then drop the temperature to 480°F (248°C) and keep baking with the lid on for 10 minutes. Take the lid off, drop the temperature again to 450°F (232°C) and finish baking for 15 to 20 minutes, or until golden brown.

Remove the bread from the oven, place it on a wire rack and allow it to cool for at least 30 minutes to 1 hour before slicing into it.

spanish sourdough

In this loaf I wanted to re-create a trip to one of my absolute favorite places: Spain. I was inspired by the variety of different tapas I tried, and one of my favorites was the Spanish tortilla, which could be compared to an Italian frittata or an omelet. The thick tortilla was layered with potatoes and cheese and accompanied by roasted piquillo peppers. This is a comforting loaf of bread that is satisfyingly cheesy and rich in flavor. The potatoes and peppers are added during the first two sets of folds for better absorption and to preserve the structure of the dough. I found that by incorporating the Manchego when shaping the loaf, I'm able to evenly fold in the cubed cheese that will later melt into large cheesy pockets when baked. If you are a fan of oozing cheese like I am, this bread is best eaten warm!

yield: 2 loaves

levain

40 g (1.41 oz) high-protein wheat flour

40 g (1.41 oz) water

20 g (0.71 oz) mature starter

final mix

200 g (7.05 oz) yellow potatoes

150 g (5.29 oz) jarred piquillo peppers, drained

100 g (3.53 oz) 24-month aged Manchego cheese

350 g (12.35 oz) high-protein wheat flour

100 g (3.53 oz) all-purpose flour

340 g (11.99 oz) water

100 g (3.53 oz) levain

7 g (0.25 oz) salt

1 g (0.035 oz) dried oregano

Start by building the levain 6 to 8 hours before mixing. For more details on my sourdough method, see page 21.

For the final mix, prepare your steamed potatoes. Place a steamer basket or a colander in a large pot. Add water until it reaches 1 or 2 inches (2.5 or 5 cm) below the bottom of the basket. Put the potatoes in the basket and bring the water to a boil. Once the water is boiling, cover the pot, reduce the heat to medium and allow the potatoes to steam until you can insert a paring knife without resistance, 30 minutes. Using tongs, remove the potatoes from the steamer basket and let them rest for 5 minutes. Peel the potatoes while they are hot using a clean towel and a paring knife. Cover them loosely with plastic wrap and place them in the refrigerator to cool completely.

Dice the piquillo peppers into ¼-inch (6-mm) squares and cube the Manchego cheese and the chilled potatoes to the same size. Reserve them in the refrigerator.

During the last 60 minutes of your starter's fermentation, start the autolyse. In the bowl of a stand mixer fitted with the paddle attachment, combine the high-protein wheat flour, all-purpose flour and water until the flour is fully hydrated and there are no dry bits left. This should take no more than 2 minutes. Cover the bowl with a towel or plastic wrap and let the mixture sit at room temperature until the levain reaches peak.

Add your mature levain to the autolysed dough and, using a stand mixer fitted with the dough hook attachment, mix on low (speed 2) for 3 minutes. Increase the speed to medium-high (speed 5) and keep mixing for 5 to 8 minutes, or until the dough has gained strength and is smooth and elastic. Reduce the speed back to low (speed 2) and add the salt. Let it incorporate for 2 minutes, then turn the mixer off, cover the bowl with a towel and let the dough rest for 15 minutes in the machine before taking it out.

Place your dough into a proofing box and start the bulk proof at a temperature between 75°F and 80°F (23°C and 26°C) for 4 hours. After the first hour of bulk fermentation, proceed with laminating the dough on a damp countertop (page 23). Distribute the diced potatoes, Manchego, piquillo peppers and dried oregano throughout the stretched dough, making sure to cover the whole surface.

Keep proofing the dough for 3 more hours, performing two sets of coil folds, once every hour.

(continued)

Transfer your dough onto a lightly floured surface, divide it in two and preshape it, giving each half a round shape, rolling with the help of a dough scraper to tighten the ball. Cover them with a towel and let them rest for 45 minutes to 1 hour at room temperature or in a proofing chamber.

Flip the preshaped dough top side down on a lightly floured surface and proceed with shaping the batards (page 29).

Dust two 10-inch (25-cm) oval bannetons with flour and transfer the shaped loaves into the baskets, seam side up, then cover them with a towel and place them in the refrigerator for a final cold proof at 39°F (4°C) for 12 to 16 hours.

Preheat your Dutch oven to 500°F (260°C), line it with a piece of parchment paper and place the proofed loaf in the Dutch oven. Score and bake the loaf with the lid on at 500°F (260°C) for 5 minutes, then drop the temperature to 480°F (248°C) and keep baking with the lid on for 10 minutes. Take the lid off, drop the temperature again to 450°F (232°C) and finish baking for 15 to 20 minutes, or until dark golden brown.

Remove the bread from the oven, place it on a wire rack and allow it to cool for at least 30 minutes to 1 hour before slicing into it.

black barley porridge bread

Black barley is one of the whole grains that can go from field to table without being processed. The dark bran layer stays attached to the kernel, giving the grain a glossy purplish-opal color when cooked. I source whole black barley from Bench View Farms, as I prefer to crack the grains myself using a grain mill set to a coarse grind. This can also be done by pulsing the barley with a powerful food processor. I then sift the cracked grains that I cook into a porridge and reserve the fine dark sifted flour to dust the banneton proofing baskets. This adds an intense aroma, color and texture to the crust. I'm a big fan of incorporating cooked grains into my breads, and black barley is definitely a healthy and colorful addition. I also use a percentage of low-protein flour in this loaf to achieve an even chewier and soft crumb. The result is a nutty and flavorful sourdough with a rustic and satisfying crust.

yield: 2 loaves

levain

65 g (2.29 oz) high-protein wheat flour

65 g (2.29 oz) water

30 g (1.06 oz) mature starter

black barley porridge

160 g (5.64 oz) water

80 g (2.82 oz) cracked black barley

final mix

450 g (15.87 oz) high-protein bread flour

250 g (8.82 oz) all-purpose flour

50 g (1.76 oz) khorasan wheat flour

500 g (17.64 oz) water

160 g (5.64 oz) levain

15 g (0.53 oz) salt

150 g (5.29 oz) black barley porridge

Dark barley flour, sifted, for dusting

Start by building the levain 6 to 8 hours before mixing. For more details on my sourdough method, see page 21.

Begin preparing the black barley porridge. In a medium saucepan, bring the water to a gentle boil, reduce the heat and add the cracked black barley. Slowly simmer for 15 to 20 minutes, or until the mixture is thick and most of the water is absorbed. Cool the porridge in the refrigerator for 1 to 2 hours.

For the final mix, during the last 60 minutes of the levain's fermentation, start the autolyse. In the bowl of a stand mixer fitted with the paddle attachment, combine the high-protein bread flour, all-purpose flour, khorasan wheat flour and water until the flour is fully hydrated and there are no dry bits left. This should take no more than 2 minutes. Cover the bowl with a towel or plastic wrap and let the mixture sit at room temperature until the levain reaches peak.

Add your mature levain to the autolysed dough and, using a stand mixer fitted with the dough hook attachment, mix on low (speed 2) for 3 minutes. Increase the speed to medium-high (speed 5) and keep mixing for 5 to 8 minutes, or until the dough has gained strength and is smooth and elastic. Reduce the speed back to low (speed 2) and add the salt. Let it incorporate for 2 minutes, then turn the mixer off, cover the bowl with a towel and let the dough rest for 15 minutes in the machine before taking it out.

Place your dough into a proofing box and start the bulk proof at a temperature between 75°F and 80°F (23°C and 26°C) for 4 hours, performing three sets of coil folds, once every hour. Add the cooled porridge to the dough when performing the first coil fold and don't worry if it looks like the porridge is not evenly absorbed right away—it will distribute evenly throughout the bulk fermentation as you keep performing folds.

Transfer your dough onto a lightly floured surface, divide it in two and preshape it, giving each half a round shape by rolling with the help of a dough scraper to tighten the ball. Cover them with a towel and let them rest for 45 minutes at room temperature or in a proofing chamber.

(continued)

black barley porridge bread (continued)

Flip the preshaped dough top side down onto a lightly floured surface and proceed with shaping the batards (page 29).

Dust two 10-inch (25-cm) oval bannetons with the sifted dark barley flour and transfer the shaped loaves into their baskets, seam side up. Place them in the refrigerator for a cold proof at 39°F (4°C) for 12 to 16 hours.

Preheat your Dutch oven to 500°F (260°C), line it with a piece of parchment paper and place the loaf in the Dutch oven. Bake the loaf with the lid on at 500°F (260°C) for 10 minutes, drop the temperature to 450°F (232°C) and keep baking with the lid on for 10 minutes. Take the lid off, drop the temperature again to 430°F (215°C) and finish baking for 15 to 20 minutes, or until dark brown.

Remove the bread from the oven, place it on a wire rack and allow it to cool for at least 30 minutes to 1 hour before slicing into it.

Enriched Breads

In this chapter, I want to share with you the brioche recipes that I have perfected over the years. We will also explore the different flavor profiles and various techniques that will take your brioche to the next level, like one of my favorite recipes in the chapter, the Sun-Dried Tomato and Olive Babka (page 94). I personally love working with brioche dough for its versatility. Virtually all of the enriched recipes in this chapter can be adapted and transformed into different bread shapes, like braids, twists, rolls, buns and loaves. If you're feeling adventurous enough, you may also laminate your brioche dough with a butter sheet following the croissant method (page 151). This will create a soft and extremely rich dough that you could use to make croissants, as well as pain au chocolate, pain au raisin or Danishes, or shape it into your favorite pastry.

The majority of the recipes in this chapter will use commercial yeast to preserve the sweetness and delicateness of this type of bread, but I also included a Sourdough Olive Oil Brioche (page 90). This recipe melds together the flavor of natural yeast with the acidity of the extra virgin olive oil that still preserves all of the distinct characteristics of a brioche bread. Enriched breads are rich, soft, slightly sweet and very good vessels for other flavors. Once you master my brioche recipe and feel comfortable enough to experiment on your own, there will be infinite ways you can transform this delicious dough.

brioche buns

There are few things I believe are more satisfying than pulling a tray of brioche buns out of the oven to find them perfectly plump and gleaming. These buns are both light and rich thanks to the substantial percentage of butter in the dough that makes them extremely soft and flavorful. With or without a dusting of sesame seeds on top, they are guaranteed to impress your guests at your next barbecue. The challenge with making any brioche recipe is incorporating the butter properly without overheating the dough, which is why I suggest always using a digital thermometer to constantly monitor the temperature. It's important that the butter is soft but not melted to facilitate its absorption into the dough. If you are having difficulty incorporating butter when using a dough hook with a small stand mixer, I suggest you switch to the paddle attachment for this step and mix for a few minutes or just until the butter is incorporated.

yield: 12 buns

100 g (3.53 oz) unsalted butter

235 g (8.29 oz) whole milk

400 g (14.11 oz) high-protein wheat flour

100 g (3.53 oz) all-purpose flour

120 g (4.23 oz) whole eggs (2 large)

50 g (1.76 oz) sugar

16 g (0.56 oz) baker's yeast

12 g (0.42 oz) salt

egg wash

1 whole egg

1 egg yolk

15 g (0.53 oz) whole milk

optional

Sesame seeds

Begin by softening the unsalted butter at room temperature for at least 2 hours, or pull it from the fridge the night before.

Using a stand mixer fitted with the dough hook attachment, mix the whole milk, high-protein wheat flour, all-purpose flour, whole eggs, sugar, baker's yeast and salt on low (speed 2) for 3 minutes. Increase the speed to medium-high (speed 6) and keep mixing for 8 to 10 minutes, or until the dough has gained strength and is smooth and elastic. Reduce the speed back to low (speed 3) and add the softened butter. Let it incorporate until it is fully absorbed—this will take a few minutes. Monitor the temperature of your brioche dough with a digital thermometer; it should not exceed 78°F (26°C) at any point. Once the butter is fully incorporated, let the dough rest in the mixer for 10 minutes before taking it out.

Pick up the dough, give it a smooth round shape by folding it into itself a couple of times, then place it into a bowl. Proof your brioche for 60 to 90 minutes at a temperature between 75°F and 80°F (24°C and 26°C). The dough should double in size.

note: If your dough overheats while mixing, exceeding the indicated temperature, and does not feel smooth and elastic, immediately turn the mixer off and let the dough sit in the bowl for 10 minutes. Before transferring it into the proofing box, pick the dough up, fold it into itself and repeat this step again halfway through proofing to help the dough strengthen.

Preheat your oven to 360°F (182°C), then transfer your brioche dough to a countertop surface and, with the help of a dough scraper, portion it into 85-gram (3-oz) pieces. Shape each piece into a tight ball by rolling it with the palm of your hand and gently pressing it against the counter as you roll it. Place the shaped bun on a sheet tray lined with parchment paper or a silicone mat.

(continued)

brioche buns (continued)

Proof the shaped buns for 60 to 90 minutes at room temperature. Cover the buns loosely with sheets of plastic wrap, making sure there are no gaps in between the sheets and the tray is completely covered to avoid your dough drying out.

For the egg wash, whisk together the whole egg, egg yolk and whole milk and gently brush the top of your buns, sprinkle them with sesame seeds, if using, and bake them for 15 to 20 minutes, or until golden brown.

Cool the buns at room temperature and store them in an airtight plastic bag in the refrigerator for up to a week or freeze them for longer storage.

Gently press the dough against the surface with the palm of your hand and, in a circular motion, roll until smooth.

As you form the buns, make sure the dough is evenly rolled and tucked underneath.

The shaped bun should be tight and smooth; make sure not to roll it excessively to avoid ripping the surface.

sourdough english muffins

This English muffin recipe isn't technically an enriched dough itself, but I wanted to include it in this chapter because the dough is fried in butter, making the muffin texturally rich and almost resembling the flavor profile of an enriched bread. The addition of whole wheat as well as a prefermented portion of the flour in both the poolish and sourdough starter builds an extraordinary amount of flavor in the dough. The use of clarified butter is fundamental when frying the English muffins. The water and milk solids removed from the butter raise the smoking point of the butterfat, making it more stable for a longer period of time when heated. Traditionally, English muffins are sprinkled with cornmeal to prevent them from sticking while proofing and to create a more rustic crust. This step is optional; I prefer using a small amount of finer semolina instead of cornmeal to get a more even and homogeneous crust.

yield: 6–8 english muffins

poolish

50 g (1.76 oz) high-protein wheat flour

50 g (1.76 oz) water

0.5 g (0.02 oz) baker's yeast

final mix

150 g (5.29 oz) all-purpose flour

75 g (2.65 oz) high-protein wheat flour

25 g (0.88 oz) whole wheat flour

125 g (4.41 oz) water

100 g (3.53 oz) poolish

75 g (2.65 oz) mature starter

10 g (0.35 oz) salt

for dusting

Semolina or cornmeal

clarified butter

120 g (4.23 oz) unsalted butter

Start by mixing the poolish the day before. Early in the afternoon, combine the high-protein wheat flour, water and baker's yeast in a bowl and mix with a spoon or by hand until all the flour is fully hydrated and there are no dry bits left. Transfer the mixture into a plastic container or leave it in the bowl and proof it for 3 to 5 hours, preferably at a temperature between 75°F and 80°F (23°C and 26°C), covered with a lid or wrapped in plastic. After proofing at room temperature, place the poolish in the refrigerator to ferment overnight for 12 hours.

Proceed by feeding your sourdough starter 3 to 4 hours before mixing.

For the final mix, during the last 60 minutes of the starter fermentation, begin the autolyse. In the bowl of a stand mixer fitted with the paddle attachment, combine the all-purpose flour, high-protein wheat flour, whole wheat flour and water until the flour is fully hydrated and there are no dry bits left. This should take no more than 2 minutes. Cover the bowl with a towel or plastic wrap and let the mixture sit at room temperature until the starter reaches peak.

Incorporate the poolish and mature starter into the autolysed dough and, using a stand mixer fitted with the dough hook attachment, mix on low (speed 2) for 3 minutes. Increase the speed to medium-high (speed 5) and keep mixing for 5 to 8 minutes, or until the dough has gained strength and is smooth and elastic. Reduce the speed back to low (speed 2) and add the salt. Let it incorporate for 2 minutes, then turn the mixer off, cover the bowl with a towel and let the dough rest for 15 minutes in the machine before taking it out.

Wet your hands before picking up the dough and use a circular motion to fold it into itself a few times, tightening it into a smooth round ball. Transfer the dough into a proofing box and bulk proof for 3 hours, performing two sets of coil folds (page 26), once every hour.

Line a large sheet tray, dust it with cornmeal or semolina and proceed with rolling the dough out onto a floured surface.

Flatten the dough with your hands into a rectangular shape and use a heavy rolling pin to roll it to 1 inch (2.5 cm) thick. Transfer the rolled dough onto the sheet tray and dust the top with semolina or cornmeal.

(continued)

Proof the dough at a temperature between 75°F and 80°F (24°C and 26°C) for 2 hours, then cover the tray with a towel and place it in the refrigerator for 2 hours. This will help the dough harden when exposed to the cold temperature, which will facilitate cutting and preserve the round shape while transferring the English muffins from the tray to the hot skillet.

While your dough rests in the fridge, prepare the clarified butter that you will use to fry the English muffins. Melt the unsalted butter over low heat in a small saucepan. You want to make sure the butter doesn't boil but instead melts extremely slowly so that the milk solids will gently separate from the fat and float to the surface. Using a spoon, gently skim off the foamy milk solids that rise to the top, then ladle the butterfat from the saucepan into a second clean saucepan or another vessel for holding. Be sure to leave the layer of water that separates from the fat in the bottom of the original saucepan.

Pull your dough from the fridge and preheat a cast-iron skillet over medium-low heat. Cut your English muffins using a 3½-inch (9-cm) ring cutter and drop a spoonful of clarified butter into the hot skillet.

Fry the muffins for 2 to 4 minutes per side, or until golden brown, and transfer them onto a wire rack to slightly cool before cutting them open.

pain de mie

Pain de mie means "bread of mostly crumb" in French. This name comes from the shape of the loaf. The typical pan used to bake this bread is called a pullman loaf pan and has a lid that slides on the top, trapping the loaf inside. As the bread bakes and rises to the top, it fills up the pan, taking the shape of a perfect square with very little crust and almost all crumb. If you don't have a pan designed for this type of bread, you may use a loaf pan with a greased sheet tray laid on top and weighted down by a small skillet to achieve the flat square shape typical of a pain de mie. Texturally extremely soft and chewy, the flavorful slices of this bread are perfect for a sandwich or toast. This recipe can also be enriched by the addition of seeds and whole grains to make a more nutritious and unique loaf.

yield: 1 loaf

125 g (4.41 oz) unsalted butter

500 g (17.64 oz) high-protein wheat flour

125 g (4.41 oz) all-purpose flour

190 g (6.7 oz) whole milk

100 g (3.53 oz) water

120 g (4.23 oz) whole eggs (2 large)

75 g (2.65 oz) sugar

22 g (0.78 oz) baker's yeast

15 g (0.53 oz) salt

Begin by softening the unsalted butter at room temperature for at least 2 hours, or pull it from the fridge the night before.

Using a stand mixer fitted with the dough hook attachment, mix the high-protein wheat flour, all-purpose flour, whole milk, water, whole eggs, sugar, baker's yeast and salt on low (speed 2) for 3 minutes. Increase the speed to medium-high (speed 5) and keep mixing for 8 to 10 minutes, or until the dough has gained strength and is smooth and elastic. Reduce the speed back to low (speed 3) and add the softened butter. Let it incorporate until it is fully absorbed—this will take a few minutes. Monitor the temperature of your brioche with a digital thermometer. It should not exceed 78°F (26°C) at any point. Once the butter is fully incorporated, let the dough rest in the mixer for 10 minutes before taking it out.

With wet hands, pick up the dough and give it a smooth round shape by folding it into itself a couple of times, then place it into a bowl. Proof the dough for 60 to 90 minutes at a temperature between 75°F and 80°F (24°C and 26°C). The dough should double in size.

> **note:** If your dough overheats while mixing and exceeds the indicated temperature and does not feel smooth and elastic, immediately turn the mixer off and let the dough sit in the bowl for 10 minutes. Before transferring it into the proofing box, pick the dough up, fold it into itself and repeat this step again halfway through proofing to help the dough strengthen.

Preheat your oven to 365°F (182°C) and butter a 9 x 4 x 4–inch (23 x 10 x 10–cm) loaf pan, then proceed with your shaping.

Transfer your brioche dough onto a countertop surface and gently flatten the dough into a rectangular shape and shape it as a simple loaf (page 29).

After the dough is shaped, pinch the seams to seal the edges and roll the loaf gently into an even shape. Transfer it into the pan, cover it with plastic wrap and proof it for 60 to 90 minutes at a temperature between 75°F and 80°F (24°C and 26°C), or until the loaf reaches just below the lip of the pan.

Slide the lid on the pan and bake the loaf for 20 minutes. Take the lid off and finish baking for 15 to 20 minutes, or until a digital thermometer reads a core temperature of 195°F (90°C).

Remove the pan from the oven and slide the loaf out of the pan and onto a wire rack. Allow it to cool for at least 1 to 2 hours before slicing into it.

sourdough olive oil brioche

This brioche recipe incorporates extra virgin olive oil to enrich this loaf with a smooth and acidic finish. Remember to always source a quality extra virgin olive oil so that the flavor shines through sharply. If you would like to experiment with a milder flavor in your brioche, substitute the extra virgin olive oil for 100 g (3.53 oz) of unsalted butter. I opted to use natural yeast in this recipe to increase the acidity and the overall texture, creating a soft and chewy consistency with a uniquely crunchy crust. The brioche is divided and shaped into four sections that are then proofed and baked in a pan laying directly against each other. When baked they will form one loaf but with distinct sections, allowing you and your family or guests the enjoyment of pulling away portions to eat.

yield: 1 loaf

150 g (5.29 oz) mature starter

200 g (7.05 oz) whole milk

500 g (17.64 oz) high-protein wheat flour

180 g (6.35 oz) whole eggs (3 large eggs)

40 g (1.41 oz) sugar

10 g (0.35 oz) salt

60 g (2.12 oz) extra virgin olive oil

Begin by feeding your starter with equal parts water and flour 3 to 4 hours before mixing. For more details on my sourdough method, see page 21.

Using a stand mixer fitted with the dough hook attachment, mix the mature starter, whole milk, high-protein wheat flour, whole eggs and sugar on low (speed 2) for 3 minutes. Increase the speed to medium-high (speed 5) and keep mixing for 8 to 10 minutes, or until the dough has gained strength and is smooth and elastic. Reduce the speed back to low (speed 2) and add the salt. Let it incorporate for 2 minutes, then slowly add the extra virgin olive oil. Let the oil incorporate into the dough until it is fully absorbed—this will take a few minutes. Monitor the temperature of your brioche with a digital thermometer; it should not exceed 78°F (26°C) at any point. Once the extra virgin olive oil is fully incorporated, let the dough rest in the mixer for 15 minutes before taking it out.

Pick up the dough and give it a smooth round shape by folding it into itself a couple of times, then place it into a bowl. Bulk proof the dough for 6 hours at a temperature between 75°F and 80°F (24°C and 26°C), performing four sets of coil folds (page 26), once every hour for the first 4 hours.

note: If your dough overheats while mixing, exceeding the above indicated temperature, and does not feel smooth and elastic, immediately turn the mixer off and let the dough sit in the bowl for 10 minutes. After transferring it into the proofing box, pick the dough up, fold it into itself and repeat this step again halfway through proofing to help the dough strengthen.

Coat a 9 x 4 x 4–inch (23 x 10 x 10–cm) loaf pan with extra virgin olive oil, then transfer the dough onto a countertop surface and divide it into four equal parts.

Shape each of the four segments by rolling them into a tight ball and place them into the pan laying against each other. Cover them with plastic wrap and proof them for 2 to 3 hours at a temperature between 75°F and 80°F (24°C and 26°C).

While your brioche proofs, preheat your oven to 410°F (210°C). When ready to bake, brush the top of the loaf with extra virgin olive oil and bake it for 25 to 35 minutes, or until a digital thermometer reads a core temperature of 190°F (88°C).

Remove the pan from the oven and slide the loaf out of the pan and onto a wire rack. Allow it to cool for at least 30 minutes to 1 hour before slicing into it.

whole grain brioche

A traditional brioche has a rich and light texture. In this case, the addition of whole grain elevates the flavor and adds not only nutritional value but also a firmer texture and structure to this loaf. This is a heartier brioche with a darker golden hue, perfectly suited for a whole grain French toast or simply enjoyed warm. I wanted to create a formula here that will also allow you to try different styles of brioche with the nutritional benefit of using whole grain. The shape of this dough can be modified in a variety of ways. For example, it can easily be shaped into single pull-apart dinner rolls and baked in a shallow pan or rolled into whole grain cinnamon rolls. You can also incorporate different flavors, including nuts and presoaked dried fruit.

yield: 1 loaf

90 g (3.17 oz) unsalted butter

320 g (11.29 oz) high-protein wheat flour

100 g (3.53 oz) all-purpose flour

80 g (2.82 oz) whole wheat flour

25 g (0.88 oz) wheat germ

130 g (4.59 oz) water

130 g (4.59 oz) whole milk

60 g (2.12 oz) whole egg (1 large)

60 g (2.12 oz) sugar

12 g (0.42 oz) salt

Coarse wheat bran, for coating

egg wash

1 whole egg

1 egg yolk

15 g (0.53 oz) whole milk

Begin by softening the unsalted butter at room temperature for at least 2 hours, or pull it from the fridge the night before.

Using a stand mixer fitted with the dough hook attachment, mix the high-protein wheat flour, all-purpose flour, whole wheat flour, wheat germ, water, whole milk, whole egg, sugar and salt on low (speed 2) for 3 minutes. Increase the speed to medium-high (speed 5) and keep mixing for 8 to 10 minutes, or until the dough has gained strength and is smooth and elastic. Reduce the speed back to low (speed 3) and add the softened butter. Let it incorporate until it is fully absorbed—this will take a few minutes. Monitor the temperature of your brioche with a digital thermometer. It should not exceed 78°F (26°C) at any point. Once the butter is fully incorporated, let the dough rest in the mixer for 10 minutes before taking it out.

With your hands wet, pick up the dough and give it a smooth round shape by folding it into itself a couple of times, then place it into a bowl. Proof the dough for 60 to 90 minutes at a temperature between 75°F and 80°F (24°C and 26°C). The dough should double in size.

note: If your dough overheats while mixing, exceeding the above indicated temperature, and does not feel smooth and elastic, immediately turn the mixer off and let the dough sit in the bowl for 10 minutes. After transferring it into the proofing box, pick the dough up, fold it into itself and repeat this step again halfway through proofing to help the dough strengthen.

Preheat your oven to 365°F (182°C) and butter a 9 x 4 x 4–inch (23 x 10 x 10–cm) loaf pan, then proceed with shaping your loaf. Transfer your brioche dough onto a countertop surface and gently flatten the dough into a rectangular shape. Pull the sides of the dough and fold them over the center, then pull the top of the dough and fold it over the center. Keep rolling the dough toward you until the seam is underneath.

Roll and form the loaf into an even shape, then transfer it into the pan, cover it with plastic wrap and proof it for 60 to 90 minutes at a temperature between 75°F and 80°F (24°C and 26°C), or until the loaf reaches just below the lip of the pan.

For the egg wash, whisk together the whole egg, egg yolk and whole milk and gently brush the top of your brioche, sprinkle it generously with coarse wheat bran and bake it for 25 to 30 minutes, or until golden brown and the internal temperature reads 195°F (90°C).

Remove the pan from the oven and slide the loaf out of the pan and onto a wire rack. Allow it to cool for at least 30 minutes to 1 hour before slicing into it.

sun-dried tomato and olive babka

Babka is without a doubt the most versatile recipe I have perfected since I started baking. The possibilities with this bread are truly endless. Sweet or savory, you can fill it with your favorite flavor combinations for a unique and fun experience every time. In this particular version, I wanted to create a rich and flavorful loaf featuring Mediterranean flavors. The babka is filled with a gorgeous sun-dried tomato pesto that, when combined with the fruity Kalamata olives, adds a salty and savory punch of flavor to every bite. The technique used to twist babka creates a beautiful loaf that is even more impressive once it is sliced.

yield: 1 loaf

brioche dough

65 g (2.29 oz) unsalted butter, plus more for greasing the pan

220 g (7.76 oz) whole milk

60 g (2.12 oz) whole egg (1 large)

50 g (1.76 oz) sugar

445 g (15.7 oz) high-protein wheat flour

12 g (0.42 oz) baker's yeast

10 g (0.35 oz) salt

sun-dried tomato pesto

50 g (1.76 oz) pine nuts

80 g (2.82 oz) jarred sun-dried tomatoes in olive oil, drained

130 g (4.59 oz) extra virgin olive oil

15 large basil leaves

2 cloves garlic

3 g (0.11 oz) salt

50 g (1.76 oz) grated Parmigiano Reggiano

30 g (1.06 oz) grated Pecorino Romano

filling

Sun-dried tomato pesto

5 g (0.18 oz) dried oregano

160 g (5.64 oz) Kalamata olives, pitted and halved

Begin by softening the butter at room temperature for at least 2 hours, or pull it from the fridge the night before.

Using a stand mixer fitted with the dough hook attachment, mix the whole milk, egg, sugar, high-protein wheat flour, baker's yeast and salt on low (speed 2) for 3 minutes. Increase the speed to medium-high (speed 5) and keep mixing for 8 to 10 minutes, or until the dough has gained strength and is smooth and elastic. Reduce the speed back to low (speed 3) and add the softened butter, letting it incorporate until it is fully absorbed—this will take a few minutes. Monitor the temperature of your brioche with a digital thermometer. It should not exceed 78°F (26°C) at any point. Once the butter is fully incorporated, let the dough rest in the mixer for 10 minutes before taking it out.

Pick up the dough and give it a smooth round shape by folding it into itself a couple of times, then place it in a bowl. Proof the dough for 60 to 90 minutes at a temperature between 75°F and 80°F (24°C and 26°C) as indicated in the Master Sourdough Method (page 22). The dough should double in size.

> **note:** If your dough overheats while mixing, exceeding the above indicated temperature, and does not feel smooth and elastic, immediately turn the mixer off and let the dough sit in the bowl for 10 minutes. After transferring it into the proofing box, pick the dough up, fold it into itself and repeat this step again halfway through proofing to help the dough strengthen.

Transfer your brioche dough to a lightly floured surface and with the help of a rolling pin roll it into a ¼-inch (6-mm)-thick rectangle. Transfer the dough onto a sheet tray lined with parchment paper. Cover it with plastic wrap and place it in the refrigerator for 1 hour.

While your brioche cools down, begin making the sun-dried tomato pesto. Preheat your oven to 320°F (160°C), then toast the pine nuts on a sheet tray for 8 to 10 minutes, or until lightly colored and fragrant. Set them aside.

To a food processor add the sun-dried tomatoes, extra virgin olive oil, fresh basil leaves, garlic and salt. Blend it for 3 to 5 minutes, or until smooth, then add the grated Parmigiano Reggiano, grated Pecorino Romano and toasted pine nuts. Keep blending for 2 more minutes, or until the mixture is smooth. Pour the pesto into a container and reserve it in the fridge.

(continued)

Butter a 10 × 5–inch (23 × 12–cm) loaf pan.

Pull your brioche dough from the refrigerator and roll it into a ¼-inch (6-mm)-thick rectangle. Trim ½ inch (1.3 cm) of dough off the edges and with an offset spatula spread all of the pesto evenly throughout the rectangle up to the edges. Sprinkle the rectangle with the dried oregano and halved Kalamata olives and, starting with the long side, roll the dough into a tight coil (see the step-by-step photos on the next page).

With a sharp knife, cut and split the rolled dough in half lengthwise to expose the filling, cross the two halves to form the letter X, then twist them together into a braid. Place the shaped babka into the buttered loaf pan and proof it for 1 hour at a temperature between 75°F and 80°F (24°C and 26°C) as indicated in the Master Sourdough Method (page 22), or until almost doubled in size.

Preheat your oven to 360°F (182°C). Bake your babka for 20 to 25 minutes, or until golden. Slide the loaf out of the pan and onto a wire rack and let it cool for 30 minutes before slicing into it.

> **note:** You can save the trimmed edges of the rolled dough and reshape them into small buns or tie them into fritters and proof them with your babka. Then either bake them with the babka or deep fry them at 350°F (176°C) in vegetable oil until golden.

shaping a babka

Spread an even layer of pesto over the whole surface of the dough, add olives and sprinkle the dried oregano before rolling.

Roll into a tight coil, starting from the long side.

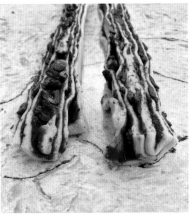

Cut the roll in half lengthwise with a sharp knife.

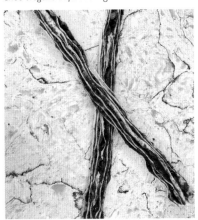

Cross the two halves.

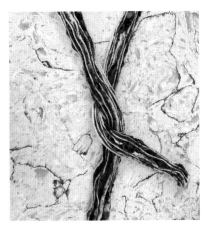

Twist one side.

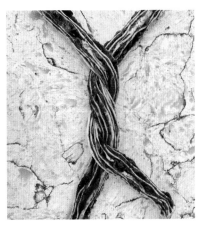

Twist the opposite side.

Continue twisting until the babka is formed.

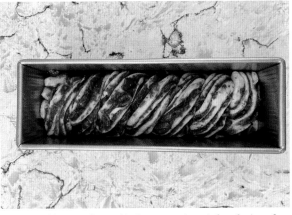

Place the babka into a buttered loaf pan to get it ready for a final proof.

Rye Bread and Pan Loaves

One of the most unique grains to me is rye. Largely used in northern and eastern European breads, this grain creates some of the most iconic pan loaves adopted all over the globe today. Rye has very different characteristics than other types of wheat: It's lower in protein and higher in minerals and vitamins, making this grain more nutritious than its close relatives. When I started playing around with rye, I was fascinated by the amount of flavor and acidity this grain develops in bread. It's very versatile and can be easily added in moderate quantities to any of your favorite bakes to elevate the flavor and texture. I'm also a big fan of pan loaves, which is why I wanted to dedicate a section to this style of bread. The hearty, rustic and earthy loaves I designed for this chapter are meant to be texturally rich and satisfying. The addition of seeds, nuts and sprouted grains in these breads enhances their complexity in addition to improving the health benefits and elevating the overall flavor.

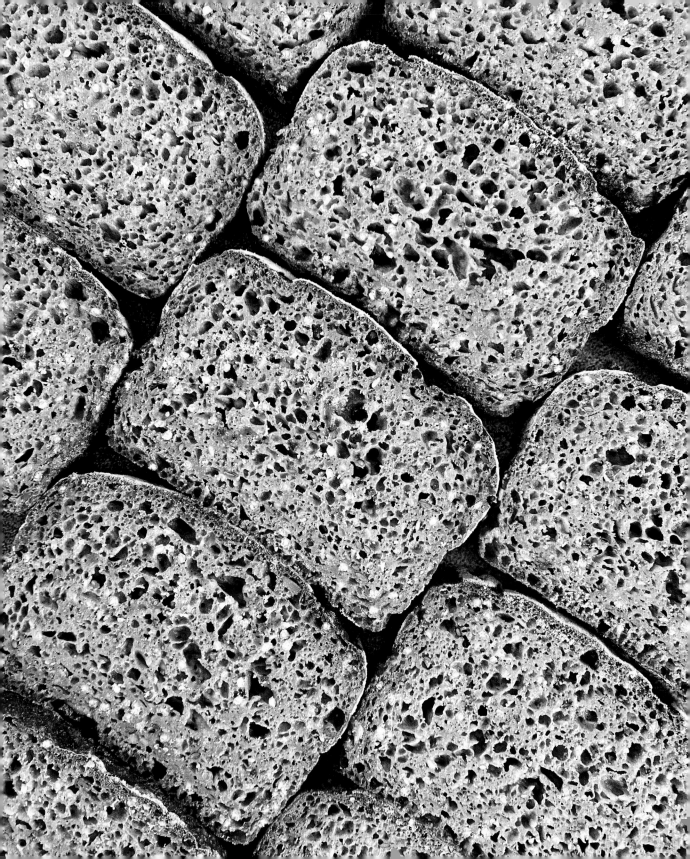

brown ale seeded rye

This loaf incorporates brown ale beer in addition to water to increase the depth of flavor and promote fermentation. This dough is made with a high percentage of rye flour and develops a soft and creamy consistency given the low protein content in the grain. In addition, the spelt flour adds silkiness to the overall texture. I suggest you mix this bread by hand, as the tactile connection to the lush consistency of the dough is extremely satisfying. Rye naturally increases the acidity of the bake, and this combined with the yogurt, beer and sourdough in this bread results in a highly acidic and rich loaf. I suggest the use of a brown ale here. With the craft brew scene continuing to grow, there are endless possibilities for you to explore different types of beers and flavor profiles. This recipe also includes presoaked seeds, which will add additional texture and nutritional value. I suggest you soak the seeds with the same beer used in the dough to add further depth of flavor.

yield: 2 loaves

seed mix

40 g (1.41 oz) of each

Rolled oats

Millet

Cracked rye

Crushed buckwheat

25 g (0.88 oz) of each

Red quinoa

White quinoa

Flax seeds

White sesame seeds

Amaranth

20 g (0.71 oz) of each

Caraway seeds

Cumin seeds

Fennel seeds

300 g (10.58 oz) brown ale beer

levain

30 g (1.06 oz) medium rye flour

30 g (1.06 oz) spelt flour

45 g (1.59 oz) water

55 g (1.94 oz) mature starter

final mix

350 g (12.35 oz) medium rye flour

150 g (5.29 oz) spelt flour

300 g (10.58 oz) water

120 g (4.23 oz) brown ale beer

75 g (2.65 oz) whole milk yogurt

10 g (0.35 oz) dark honey

160 g (5.64 oz) levain

160 g (5.64 oz) seed mix

10 g (0.35 oz) salt

Begin by soaking 160 grams (5.64 oz) of the seed mix with 300 grams (10.58 oz) of brown ale beer in a plastic container. Stir and let sit overnight at room temperature covered with a lid or a kitchen towel. Any excess seed mix can be saved in an airtight container for future use.

The next day, build the levain 3 to 4 hours before mixing. For more details on my sourdough method, see page 21.

For the final mix, once the levain reaches peak, in a large bowl, mix by hand the medium rye flour and spelt flour with the water, brown ale beer, yogurt and dark honey until all the liquids are absorbed and there are no dry bits left. The mixture should be smooth and creamy.

Add your mature levain to the mix by hand until it is fully incorporated. This should take 6 to 8 minutes. Drain the seed mix from the soaking liquid and add it to the dough followed by the salt and mix for 3 to 5 minutes, or until fully incorporated.

The dough should look wet and a lot softer than a typical wheat sourdough at this point.

(continued)

With the help of a dough scraper, clean the sides of the bowl to gather any residual bits of dough, cover the bowl with plastic wrap and start the bulk proof at a temperature between 75°F and 80°F (23°C and 26°C) for 4 hours, performing three sets of folds every 45 minutes.

note: Given the creamy dough texture, you won't be able to stretch and fold as you normally would with a classic sourdough. I suggest you dip your hands in water, pick up one side of the dough and fold it over and onto itself. Repeat folding each side of the dough over the top.

Butter two 9 x 5–inch (23 x 12–cm) loaf pans and with wet hands, scoop up half of the dough and fill the pans right below the lip, then with a wet, flexible dough scraper, smooth the top.

Cover the pans with a towel and place them in the refrigerator for a final cold proof at 39°F (4°C) for 12 to 16 hours.

Preheat the oven to 425°F (218°C). Bake the loaves for 1 hour and 10 minutes, or until the internal temperature reads 210°F (99°C).

Remove the bread from the oven and slide the loaves from the pans and onto a wire rack. Allow your rye bread to cool for at least 30 minutes to 1 hour before slicing into it.

sprouted purple barley

This recipe requires you to plan ahead a few days and give yourself time to sprout the grains properly to get the most flavor and nutrition out of them. Sprouting grains is a labor of love, but the outcome is oh so satisfying. This process allows the grain to be more easily digestible as the germination breaks down some of the starch, making the nutrients more accessible. I'm a huge fan of adding sprouted grains into my loaves not just for their health benefits but also for the amazing flavor they add to the bread. Make sure you source hull-less barley instead of pearled or hulled barley where the germ has been damaged during processing to the point that it will no longer sprout. Once you master this loaf, I suggest you substitute barley for other grains using this same formula and experiment with sprouting different grains.

yield: 1 loaf

180 g (6.35 oz) sprouted purple barley

730 g (25.75 oz) water, divided

430 g (15.17 oz) high-protein wheat flour

20 g (0.71 oz) emmer wheat flour

90 g (3.17 oz) mature starter

10 g (0.35 oz) salt

Begin by sprouting your purple barley. The sprouting process will take a few days, so you should plan this bake in advance.

Using a fine-mesh colander, rinse your purple barley under cold running water for a few minutes, then combine it with 400 grams (14.11 oz) of water in a glass jar or plastic container and soak it at room temperature for 8 to 12 hours. The next day, drain the grains and place them in a large mason jar. Secure a cheesecloth or a double layer of paper towels tightly over the mouth of the jar with a rubber band or the ring of the jar lid. Turn the jar upside down over your sink so that the excess water can drain and leave the grains for 2 to 3 days, rinsing and draining them a few times a day. Once sprouted, you may store your grains in the refrigerator for up to a week.

Now that your grains are sprouted, feed your starter with equal parts water and flour 3 to 4 hours before mixing. For more details on my sourdough method, see page 21.

During the last 60 minutes of your starter's fermentation, begin the autolyse. In the bowl of a stand mixer fitted with the paddle attachment, combine the high-protein wheat flour, emmer wheat flour and 330 grams (11.64 oz) of water until the flour is fully hydrated and there are no dry bits left. This should take no more than 2 minutes. Cover the bowl with a towel or plastic wrap and let the mixture sit at room temperature until the starter reaches peak.

Incorporate your starter into the autolysed dough and, using a stand mixer fitted with the dough hook attachment, mix on low (speed 2) for 3 minutes. Increase the speed to medium-high (speed 5) and keep mixing for 5 to 8 minutes, or until the dough has gained strength and is smooth and elastic. Reduce the speed back to low (speed 2) and add the salt. Let it incorporate for 2 minutes, then turn the mixer off, cover the bowl with a towel and let the dough rest for 15 minutes in the machine before taking it out.

Place your dough into a proofing box and start the bulk proof at a temperature between 75°F and 80°F (23°C and 26°C) for 4 hours, performing three sets of coil folds, once every hour.

Add the sprouted grains during the first set of coil folds. Don't worry if it looks like the grains don't absorb evenly into the dough at the first set of folds—they will distribute evenly throughout the bulk fermentation as you keep performing folds.

(continued)

Transfer your dough onto a lightly floured surface and proceed with shaping the batard (page 29).

Transfer the shaped loaf seam side down into a 9 x 4 x 4–inch (23 x 10 x 10–cm) loaf pan, cover it with a towel and place it in the refrigerator for a final cold proof at 39°F (3.9°C) for 12 to 16 hours.

Place a deep pan filled with lava rocks at the bottom of your oven and preheat it to 460°F (237°C). Place the loaf from the fridge directly into the oven and pour a half pint (240 ml) of water onto the lava rocks to create steam in the chamber. Quickly shut the oven door and bake for 20 minutes, open the oven door just a few inches to release steam for a few seconds, then close the door again and keep baking for 20 to 30 minutes, or until golden brown.

Remove the bread from the oven, slide the loaf out of the pan and onto a wire rack and allow the loaf to cool for at least 30 minutes to 1 hour before slicing into it.

spelt rye loaf

The use of spelt flour and a lower percentage of rye makes this dough easier to handle and shape, which gives you the option of baking the loaf with or without a pan. The final dough is rolled in rye flakes, which add a rustic texture and toasted aroma to the crust. Cracked rye is soaked overnight in water and sourdough culture to kickstart fermentation and transform the cracked grain's texture and flavor. The addition of prefermented grain to this loaf creates a nutrient-rich and extremely flavorful bread. This is a technique that I find elevates my breads when adding whole grains or seeds.

yield: 2 loaves

levain

50 g (1.76 oz) high-protein wheat flour

10 g (0.35 oz) dark rye flour

60 g (2.12 oz) water

60 g (2.12 oz) mature starter

final mix

150 g (5.29 oz) cracked rye

500 g (17.64 oz) all-purpose flour

300 g (10.58 oz) spelt flour

100 g (3.53 oz) dark rye flour

650 g (22.93 oz) water

180 g (6.35 oz) levain

25 g (0.88 oz) salt

Rye flakes, for coating

Begin by soaking the cracked rye in double the amount of water and a spoonful of sourdough starter overnight at room temperature. The next day, build the levain 3 to 4 hours before mixing. For more details on my sourdough method, see page 21.

For the final mix, during the last 60 minutes of your levain fermentation, start the autolyse. In the bowl of a stand mixer fitted with the paddle attachment, combine the all-purpose flour, spelt flour, dark rye flour and water until the flour is fully hydrated and there are no dry bits left. This should take no more than 2 minutes. Cover the bowl with a towel or plastic wrap and let the mixture sit at room temperature until the levain reaches peak.

Add your levain to the autolysed dough and, using a stand mixer fitted with the dough hook attachment, mix on low (speed 2) for 3 minutes. Increase the speed to medium-high (speed 5) and keep mixing for 5 to 8 minutes, or until the dough has gained strength and is smooth and elastic. Reduce the speed back to low (speed 2) and add the salt. Let it incorporate for 2 minutes, then turn the mixer off, cover the bowl with a towel and let the dough rest for 15 minutes in the machine before taking it out.

Place your dough into a proofing box and start the bulk proof at a temperature between 75°F and 80°F (23°C and 26°C) for 4 hours, performing three sets of coil folds, once every hour.

Transfer your dough onto a lightly floured surface, divide it in two and preshape it by giving each half a round shape, rolling with the help of a dough scraper to tighten the ball. Cover them with a towel and let them rest for 1 hour at room temperature or in a proofing chamber.

Flip the preshaped dough top side down onto a lightly floured surface and proceed with shaping the boules (page 29).

Line a tray filled with rye flakes. Lightly spray the top of the shaped loaves with water before rolling each one onto the rye flakes so that the coating will adhere on the surface evenly. Line two 10-inch (25-cm) oval bannetons and transfer each loaf coated side down into the basket, then cover them with a towel and place them in the refrigerator for a final cold proof at 39°F (3.9°C) for 12 to 16 hours.

Preheat your Dutch oven to 500°F (260°C), line it with a piece of parchment paper and place the proofed loaf in the Dutch oven. Score and bake the loaf with the lid on at 500°F (260°C) for 5 minutes, drop the temperature to 480°F (248°C) and keep baking with the lid on for 10 minutes. Take the lid off, drop the temperature to 450°F (232°C) and finish baking for 15 to 20 minutes, or until dark brown.

Remove the bread from the oven, place it on a wire rack and allow it to cool for at least 30 minutes to 1 hour before slicing into it.

toasted caraway pumpernickel

A traditional pumpernickel typically uses a high percentage of dark rye flour and results in a denser, darker and heavier loaf. In this recipe, I wanted to develop a formula that brings you the flavor profile of a pumpernickel bread but with a thicker crust and a chewier crumb. Dark rye flour or pumpernickel flour is "dark" because the majority of the bran is left in when milled. Caraway seeds add a sharp and peppery note reminiscent of anise that will bring the familiar flavor that is traditionally associated with rye breads. Also, the sorghum syrup brings sweetness and a softer texture to the crumb.

yield: 2 loaves

levain

50 g (1.76 oz) high-protein wheat flour

30 g (1.06 oz) dark rye flour

80 g (2.82 oz) water

40 g (1.41 oz) mature starter

final mix

200 g (7.05 oz) pumpernickel flour or dark rye flour

600 g (21.16 oz) high-protein wheat flour

650 g (22.93 oz) water

40 g (1.41 oz) caraway seeds

200 g (7.05 oz) levain

20 g (0.71 oz) sorghum syrup

20 g (0.71 oz) salt

Start by building the levain 6 to 8 hours before mixing. For more details on my sourdough method, see page 21. For the final mix, during the last 60 minutes of your starter's fermentation, start the autolyse.

In the bowl of a stand mixer fitted with the paddle attachment, combine the pumpernickel flour, high-protein wheat flour and water until the flour is fully hydrated and there are no dry bits left. This should take no more than 2 minutes. Cover the bowl with a towel or plastic wrap and let the mixture sit at room temperature until the starter reaches peak.

Meanwhile, toast the caraway seeds in a dry skillet over medium-high heat for 2 to 3 minutes, or until fragrant. Remove them from the pan and let them cool to room temperature.

Add your mature levain and the sorghum syrup into the autolysed dough and, using a stand mixer fitted with the dough hook attachment, mix on low (speed 2) for 3 minutes. Increase the speed to medium-high (speed 5) and keep mixing for 5 to 8 minutes, or until the dough has gained strength and is smooth and elastic. Reduce the speed back to low (speed 2) and add the salt. Let it incorporate for 2 minutes, then turn the mixer off, cover the bowl with a towel and let the dough rest for 15 minutes in the machine before taking it out.

Transfer your dough into a proofing box and start the bulk proof at a temperature between 75°F and 80°F (23°C and 26°C) for 4 hours, performing three sets of coil folds, once every hour.

Transfer your dough onto a lightly floured surface, divide it in two and preshape it by giving each half a round shape, rolling with the help of a dough scraper to tighten them into a ball. Cover them with a towel and let them rest for 1 hour at room temperature or in a proofing chamber. Flip the preshaped dough top side down onto a rye floured surface and proceed with shaping the boules (page 29).

Dust two 10-inch (25-cm) round bannetons with dark rye flour and transfer each loaf into the basket, seam side up, then cover them with a towel and place them in the refrigerator for a final cold proof at 39°F (3.9°C) for 12 to 16 hours.

Preheat your Dutch oven to 500°F (260°C), line it with a piece of parchment paper and place the proofed loaf in the Dutch oven. Score the top of the loaf by making small cuts using the tip of kitchen shears and bake it with the lid on at 500°F (260°C) for 5 minutes, drop the temperature to 480°F (248°C) and keep baking with the lid on for 10 minutes. Take the lid off, drop the temperature to 450°F (232°C) and finish baking for 15 to 20 minutes, or until dark brown.

Remove the bread from the oven, place it on a wire rack and allow it to cool for at least 30 minutes to 1 hour before slicing into it.

corn polenta loaf

This loaf packs a punch of corn flavor, with both cooked corn kernels and polenta. For extra flavor, I recommend grilling your corn on the cob with the husk on to get a charred and smoky flavor. The polenta is cooked to a thick consistency to add texture and bite to the crumb. I also roll the dough in coarse cornmeal after shaping it to add a rustic finish to the crust in contrast to the soft and moist center.

yield: 1 loaf

polenta

400 g (14.11 oz) water

150 g (5.29 oz) polenta flour or corn grits

10 g (0.35 oz) extra virgin olive oil

final mix

350 g (12.35 oz) high-protein wheat flour

100 g (3.53 oz) einkorn flour

340 g (11.99 oz) water

90 g (3.17 oz) mature starter

10 g (0.35 oz) salt

220 g (7.76 oz) cooked polenta

180 g (6.35 oz) cooked corn kernels (either boiled, steamed or grilled)

Feed your starter with equal parts water and flour 3 to 4 hours before mixing. For more details on my sourdough method, see page 21.

Proceed with cooking the polenta. In a small saucepan, bring the water to a gentle boil over medium heat and gradually add the polenta flour and the extra virgin olive oil. Cook the polenta over low heat, stirring frequently for 20 to 25 minutes, or until thick and smooth. Cool it in the refrigerator covered with plastic wrap.

For the final mix, during the last 60 minutes of your starter's fermentation, start the autolyse. In the bowl of a stand mixer fitted with the paddle attachment, combine the high-protein wheat flour, einkorn flour and water until the flour is fully hydrated and there are no dry bits left. This should take no more than 2 minutes. Cover the bowl with a towel and let it sit at room temperature until the starter reaches peak.

Incorporate your starter into the autolysed dough and, using a stand mixer fitted with the dough hook attachment, mix on low (speed 2) for 3 minutes. Increase the speed to medium-high (speed 5) and keep mixing for 5 to 8 minutes, or until the dough has gained strength and is smooth and elastic. Reduce the speed back to low (speed 2) and add the salt. Let it incorporate for 2 minutes, then turn the mixer off, cover the bowl with a towel and let the dough rest for 15 minutes in the machine before taking it out.

Transfer your dough into a proofing box and start the bulk proof at a temperature between 75°F and 80°F (23°C and 26°C) for 4 hours, performing three sets of coil folds, once every hour. Add the polenta during the first set of coil folds and the corn during the second set of folds. The corn and polenta will distribute evenly throughout the bulk fermentation as you keep performing folds.

Transfer your dough onto a polenta flour–dusted surface and shape a pan loaf. Gently enlarge the dough into a rectangle, pull one side and fold it over the center then pull the opposite side and fold it over the center to meet the other folded side. Pull the top and fold it over the center and with both hands keep rolling the dough toward you until the seam is left underneath. Transfer the shaped loaf seam side down into a 9 x 4 x 4–inch (23 x 10 x 10–cm) loaf pan, cover it with a towel and place it in the refrigerator for a final cold proof at 39°F (3.9°C) for 12 to 16 hours.

Place a deep pan filled with lava rocks at the bottom of your oven and preheat it to 460°F (237°C). Score and place the polenta loaf in the oven directly from the fridge and pour a half pint (240 ml) of water onto the lava rocks to create steam in the chamber. Quickly shut the oven door and bake for 20 minutes, open the oven door just a few inches to release steam for a few seconds, then close the door and keep baking for 30 to 40 minutes, or until golden brown.

Remove the bread from the oven, slide the loaf out of the pan and onto a wire rack and allow it to cool for at least 30 minutes to 1 hour before slicing into it.

country-style muesli loaf

This loaf makes the perfect slice for breakfast or a light snack. A rich and nutty country-style muesli is soaked in apple cider for an extra layer of sweetness and then mixed with a traditional sourdough bread formula. The dough is also enriched by the addition of honey, which helps the crust brown evenly and adds flavor to the overall bread. It's fundamental to soak any grains and dry additions before incorporating them into your dough to prevent them from drawing moisture from the mix and altering the hydration. The end product is both nutritious and flavorful and will not disappoint any muesli lovers. In the fall this is a must-have loaf, toasted with a smear of apple butter.

yield: 1 loaf

180 g (6.35 oz) muesli, plus extra for coating

300 g (10.58 oz) apple cider

350 g (12.35 oz) high-protein bread flour

100 g (3.53 oz) all-purpose flour

300 g (10.58 oz) water

90 g (3.17 oz) mature starter

25 g (0.88 oz) honey

10 g (0.35 oz) salt

Begin by soaking the muesli in the apple cider and letting it sit overnight at room temperature. The next day, feed your starter with equal parts water and flour 3 to 4 hours before mixing. For more details on my sourdough method, see page 21.

During the last 60 minutes of your starter's fermentation, start the autolyse. In the bowl of a stand mixer fitted with the paddle attachment, combine the high-protein bread flour, all-purpose flour and water until the flour is fully hydrated and there are no dry bits left. This should take no more than 2 minutes. Cover the bowl with a towel or plastic wrap and let the mixture sit at room temperature until the starter reaches peak.

Incorporate your starter into the autolysed dough and, using a stand mixer fitted with the dough hook attachment, mix on low (speed 2) for 3 minutes. Add the honey and keep mixing for 2 minutes. Increase the speed to medium-high (speed 5) and keep mixing for 5 to 8 minutes, or until the dough has gained strength and is smooth and elastic. Reduce the speed back to low (speed 2) and add the salt. Let it incorporate for 2 minutes, then turn the mixer off, cover the bowl with a towel and let the dough rest for 15 minutes in the machine before taking it out.

Transfer your dough into a proofing box and start the bulk proof at a temperature between 75°F and 80°F (23°C and 26°C) for 4 hours, performing three sets of coil folds, once every hour.

Drain and add the muesli to the dough during the first set of coil folds. Don't worry if it looks like the muesli is not evenly absorbed into the dough at the first set of folds—it will distribute evenly throughout the bulk fermentation as you keep performing folds.

Line a tray filled with dry muesli, transfer your dough onto a lightly floured surface and shape a batard (page 29). Lightly spray the top of the shaped loaf with water before rolling it into the muesli so that the coating will adhere on the surface evenly.

Transfer the shaped loaf seam side down into a 9 x 4 x 4–inch (23 x 10 x 10–cm) loaf pan, cover it with a towel and place it in the refrigerator for a final cold proof at 39°F (4°C) for 12 to 16 hours.

Place a deep pan filled with lava rocks at the bottom of your oven and preheat it to 460°F (237°C). Place the loaf in the oven directly from the fridge and pour a half pint (240 ml) of water onto the lava rocks to create steam in the chamber. Quickly shut the oven door and bake for 20 minutes, open the oven door just a few inches to release steam and keep baking for 20 to 30 minutes, or until golden brown.

Remove the bread from the oven, slide the loaf out of the pan and onto a wire rack and allow it to cool for at least 30 minutes to 1 hour before slicing into it.

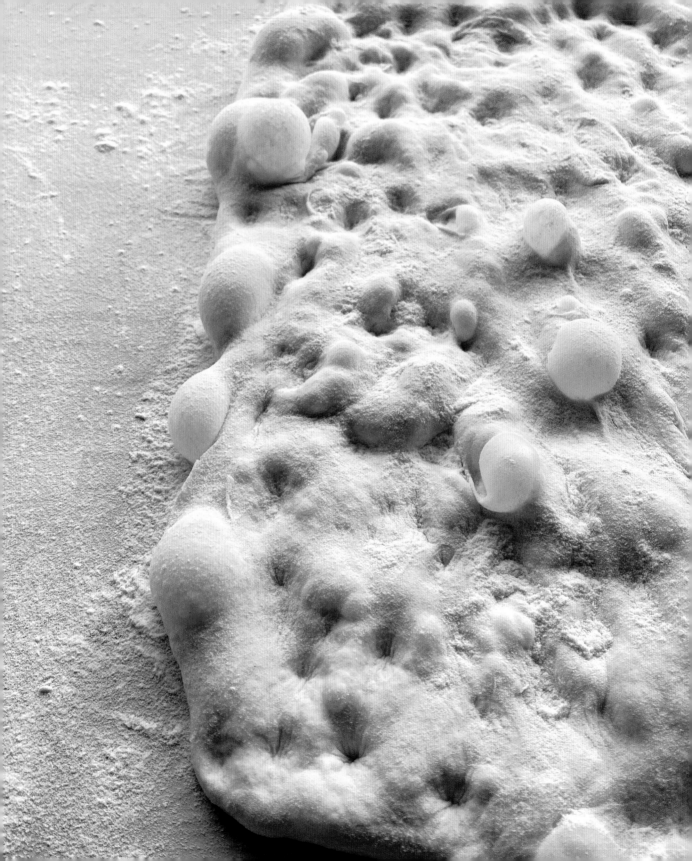

Pizza and Focaccia

If I had to choose, I would say pastries are my favorite things to bake, but pizza is without a doubt my favorite bake to eat. With this in mind, I wanted to dedicate a whole chapter to pizza and focaccia. A veil of fresh mozzarella on a perfectly seasoned tomato sauce, topped with fresh basil and all of it laying on a crunchy and airy crust is the one bite that takes me right back to my childhood. Growing up in Rome really was an opportunity for me to experience the depths of flavor that today as a chef and baker I desperately seek to achieve when working on my creations.

What's fascinating about pizza and focaccia in Italy is that every region cherishes its own traditions, and those traditions translate into the food of the area with products like wine, cheese, pasta and, of course, bread and pizza. In this section, I have captured some of my favorite styles from north to south. I wanted to re-create the most delicious variations of pizza and focaccia like the Romana, Napoletana and Pugliese, just to name a few. In this chapter, I want to share with you all the secrets I have learned over the years and equip you with the tools necessary to bake some of the best authentic pizza and focaccia you'll ever make. I'll be discussing different techniques and will show you how four simple ingredients combined in different ratios can give birth to products with completely distinct characteristics. Most importantly, every one of these recipes is absolutely delicious in its uniqueness.

the fundamentals of pizza

Before we get into the details and techniques of how to actually make pizza and focaccia, I think it is fundamental to talk about what kind of flours and ingredients you need before planning your next pizza party. Allow me to guide you through the basics of pizza making so that you have a better understanding of the process and will know exactly what to look for when sourcing your ingredients.

I strongly recommend the use of flours specifically designed for pizza making in order to achieve the best results. **The four types of flour you will need to follow the recipes in this chapter are 00, 0, 1 and semola rimacinata.** This numeric system is what is used in Italy to classify the flour strength, with the 00 being the finest and lowest in protein, usually between 10% and 12%. This is the most refined flour, where the germ and husk of the grain are removed and with them most of the nutrition. The type 0 is somewhere in between; it's higher in protein and stronger than the 00—this is a flour that could be compared to a high-protein bread flour with a protein content above 12%. The type 1 is the least refined of the three and also the most nutritious, with most of the germ and husk left in it and a very high protein content, essentially a whole wheat flour. You will notice throughout this chapter how I like to use the type 1 in small quantities in many of my pizza and focaccia doughs as it adds a great amount of flavor and texture to the crust.

All three of these flours are made from soft wheat, or what they call in Italy grano tenero, and are mainly used for pizza and pastries, whereas the hard wheat types, or grano duro, are mostly used in bread and pasta.

Semola instead comes from durum wheat and is the flour mostly known for making fresh pasta, but it is also largely used to make different regional breads in Italy. There are different denominations for semola depending on how the grain is milled, and in this chapter we will only be focusing on using the semola rimacinata, meaning "twice milled." This is the finest type and is most suitable for pizza and focaccia.

When thinking of pizza, the two main ingredients that come to mind are tomato and mozzarella cheese. Since moving to the United States years ago, I have tried making pizza sauce with many different canned tomato brands, and after trying Bianco di Napoli, I was hooked and have been using it since. They make the absolute best tomato you can ask for and you won't believe how you'll be able to elevate a simple tomato sauce by simply using the best ingredients.

Similarly, when choosing a high-quality extra virgin olive oil, you should take the same care as sourcing your flour, tomatoes and other ingredients. You want to make sure to source extra virgin, as this labeling describes a product that hasn't been refined and altered during processing. It's an oil that maintains all the characteristics and flavorful notes from the region where the olives were grown. The taste of olive oil can vary greatly based on the environment where the olive trees grow.

A simple way to immediately recognize the quality of olive oil is the color and smell. Extra virgin olive oil is high in acidity, should appear dark green in color and smell bright, peppery and earthy. I suggest avoiding olive oil that is not extra virgin or other types of oils, as they are chemically treated and stripped of any flavor and character.

for my tomato sauce

396 g (14 oz) canned whole peeled tomatoes (1 small can)

5 large fresh basil leaves

5 g (0.18 oz) salt

1 g (0.035 oz) dried oregano

35 g (1.23 oz) extra virgin olive oil

I like to use whole peeled tomatoes to get a texturally thick and rustic sauce. I usually pour the tomatoes into a bowl and crush them by squeezing them with my hands for a few minutes. **I suggest you never blend tomatoes, as you will disrupt their texture and your sauce will be too watery.** Once the mixture is roughly homogeneous, I tear the basil into small pieces and add it to the bowl followed by the salt, dried oregano and extra virgin olive oil and stir them until combined. I strongly suggest you stay away from premade pizza sauces and that you make your own sauce the day you plan on baking the pizza to get the best flavor out of it. I promise you won't regret it.

Traditionally pizza is made with mozzarella cheese. There are some recipes in this chapter, like the Quattro Formaggi, Wild Mushroom and Truffle (page 123) and the Potato and Scamorza (page 123) pizza, that will use multiple cheese options. When using mozzarella though, it is imperative to buy fresh mozzarella. I caution against using preshredded mozzarella or any blended shredded cheese mix. You will get a much more authentic and flavorful outcome by tearing fresh mozzarella to top your pizza. Keep in mind that fresh mozzarella has a higher moisture content, and if you use buffalo mozzarella, you will want to drain off any extra liquid or pat it dry prior to topping your pizza.

There are different theories and preferences with the leavening agent used for pizza. I personally prefer the use of commercial yeast, precisely baker's yeast. Pizza was made long before commercial yeast became available in the late 1800s. Despite this, I still prefer to use baker's yeast over sourdough because of the distinct flavor profile and texture that develops in the finished product. Once commercial yeast became available, virtually all bakers began using it as a leavening agent for pizza, and this created the flavor we are all nostalgic for when we pick up a slice. However, I wanted to include a sourdough pizza recipe in this chapter so that if you wish to make pizza or focaccia using natural yeast, you may adopt the Sourdough Genovese recipe (page 127) and transform it into your favorite creation.

If you would like to convert fresh yeast to dry, generally I use half the amount of active dry yeast and one-third of the amount of instant dry yeast called for in the recipe.

master pizza and focaccia method

mix

As mentioned before, the pizza and focaccia doughs in this chapter use primarily commercial yeast as a leavening agent. Because there is not much you have to do to the yeast except adding it to the mix, you will soon learn what a simple process it is to make pizza dough.

Just like we have seen in the previous chapters on sourdough bread and learned about in the Master Sourdough Method (page 21), autolyse can also be a helpful step when making pizza and focaccia to enhance the flavor and the overall structure of your dough. (More on autolyse on page 21.)

For the recipes in this chapter that use the autolyse technique, you should follow the instructions below:

Using a stand mixer, add three-quarters of the water with all of the flour called for in the recipe and mix it together with the dough hook attachment until all of the water is absorbed and there are no dry bits left. This step should take no more than a few minutes. Let the mixture sit in the bowl, covered with plastic wrap, as indicated in each recipe.

As discussed in the Master Sourdough Method (page 21), this step will improve the extensibility of your dough and will also facilitate more water absorption, which is why I start my autolyse with only a portion of the water and add the rest at a later stage of mixing, after the gluten has already formed. This allows me to take the dough to higher levels of hydration, creating a more extensible and stronger structure that is easier to work with, ultimately resulting in a pizza with a lighter crust.

After the autolyse, set the bowl in the stand mixer fitted with the dough hook attachment and start mixing on low (speed 3). Immediately add the baker's yeast and salt and keep mixing for 2 minutes. Increase the speed to medium-high (speed 5) and mix for 6 to 8 minutes, adding the remaining water slowly in small increments, making sure the dough absorbs it fully before adding more. After just a few minutes, your dough should

already appear smooth and elastic. Once all the water is fully incorporated, your dough should be silky white and smooth. If a recipe calls for extra virgin olive oil, now is the time to add it. Reduce the speed back to low (speed 3) and slowly pour in the extra virgin olive oil, let it incorporate for a few minutes until it is fully absorbed, then turn the mixer off and transfer your dough into a proofing box to start the bulk proof.

For the recipes in the chapter that do not use autolyse, I suggest you closely monitor the temperature of your ingredients depending on the temperature of your environment. To keep my dough consistent, I like to start mixing with colder water, around 40°F to 50°F (5°C to 10°C), to allow a better gluten development over the length of mixing, because the mixing time is quite long compared to a dough made with autolyse. Remember, autolysing your flour allows for enzymes to start breaking down proteins, improving gluten development and reducing mixing time. However, as mentioned in the Master Sourdough Method (page 21), this is not an absolutely necessary step and can be skipped for any of the recipes in this chapter.

Two important notes to keep in mind are that baker's yeast can be added directly to the mix without the need of being previously dissolved in water, and that I add salt at the beginning stages of mixing instead of at the end (like I do in my sourdough recipes). As mentioned in the Ingredients section (page 16), salt draws moisture from the dough and, in the case of pizza and focaccia, that is a reaction I want to happen, as it allows the flour to hydrate more slowly, which in turn tightens gluten bonds. Given the fact that I'm not using preferments like poolish or biga in the recipes of this chapter—which would add strength to the dough—adding the salt at the beginning of the mix ultimately helps me develop a stronger dough.

You always want to make sure to add the water to the mixer before your flour so that all the ingredients will incorporate evenly. Pouring water over the flour will increase the risk of leaving some of it not hydrated and stuck to the bottom of the bowl, especially if you are using a small stand mixer.

Using a stand mixer fitted with the dough hook attachment, proceed by adding three-quarters of the water to the mixing bowl, followed by all of the flour called for in the recipe. Start mixing on low (speed 2) for 2 minutes, or until all the ingredients are combined, then add the baker's yeast and salt and keep mixing for 2 minutes. Increase the speed to medium-high (speed 5) and mix for 8 to 10 minutes, adding the remaining water slowly in small increments, making sure the dough fully absorbs it before adding more. Once all the water is fully incorporated, your dough should have gained strength and appear smooth and elastic. If a recipe calls for extra virgin olive oil, now is the time to add it. Reduce the speed back to low (speed 3) and slowly pour in the extra virgin olive oil, let it incorporate for a few minutes until it is fully absorbed, then turn the mixer off and transfer your dough into a proofing box to start the bulk proof.

proof and preshape

When making pizza, the goal is to inoculate the dough with the smallest amount of yeast possible and let the dough ferment extremely slowly over a long period of time. The extended enzymatic activity during fermentation is essential to build flavor and more complex aromas as the yeast breaks down more starches and simple sugars. This produces carbon dioxide and ethanol, which is also the reason why a long-fermented pizza dough is more digestible than a quick-risen dough.

For these reasons, I choose to always extend my pizza dough fermentation in the refrigerator at 39°F (4°C) for at least 24 hours and up to 96 hours.

After mixing, have a proofing box ready that is big enough, noting that your dough will increase 50% to 70%. Once you transfer the dough into the proofing box, cover it with a lid or plastic wrap. Your dough is now ready for its long fermentation. All of the recipes in this chapter are designed for a 48-hour cold fermentation, as I find that in this amount of time, I'm able to build great flavor in my dough. I'm always happy with the results after this amount of time. I encourage you to experiment with different proofing times to have a better understanding of how time affects your final product.

There are a couple of different ways you may handle your dough from this point forward.

1. After mixing, you can let the dough ferment at room temperature covered with a lid or plastic wrap for a few hours, though I usually don't let this go on for over 4 hours. If you work with a high-hydration dough and you need to strengthen the dough, you can even perform one or two sets of coil folds, 1 to 2 hours apart. Divide your dough into the desired size and preshape it into round balls using both of your hands or with the help of a bench knife by rolling and tucking the dough into itself, just enough to create some tension, and carefully trying not to rip the surface. Transfer the preshaped dough into individual containers for focaccia dough or into a 3-inch (8-cm)-deep pizza proofing box for Margherita Napoletana (page 138) or round pizza. You want to make sure the single preshaped Napoletana pizza doughs sit in the proofing box 2 to 5 inches (5 to 12 cm) apart. Last, place the dough covered in the refrigerator for 48 hours or longer.

2. After mixing, let your dough sit in the mixer bowl for 20 minutes, then transfer it onto a countertop surface and roll it into a tight ball. Put the balled dough into a plastic container, cover it with a lid or plastic wrap and place it directly in the refrigerator to bulk ferment for 48 hours or longer.

Proceed by dividing and preshaping the dough as mentioned above right after the cold fermentation to get it ready for the final proof before baking.

Once the dough has been fermented in the refrigerator for 48 hours, either preshaped or in bulk, take it out and final proof it for 3 to 4 hours at a temperature between 75°F and 80°F (24°C and 26°C) before shaping and baking it as indicated in each recipe.

After drizzling extra virgin olive oil on the focaccia, dimple by gently pressing down with your fingertips.

Make sure to distribute pockets evenly throughout the whole surface without excessively deflating the focaccia.

shape

The main factor that differentiates pizza from focaccia is the way the dough is shaped and handled before baking. Pizza is portioned into individual pieces and proofed until they are ready to be stretched into a round shape with a thin center and a thicker edge for the traditional crusty look, then baked immediately. Focaccia is usually baked in a pan, and depending on the type, it can be proofed again after stretching and shaping. It is often dimpled to create pockets that will capture seasoning and regulate the thickness of the dough while baking to give a more homogeneous surface.

It is extremely important to bake pizza and focaccia in the right pan for even heat distribution and consistent results. I personally use different size aluminum pizza pans from LloydPans for my Roman pizza and various focaccia recipes, as I love the quality and consistency of their products.

When your dough is ready to be stretched and baked, have your pizza pan ready and dusted with semola rimacinata or greased with extra virgin olive oil, depending on the recipe. I often use semola rimacinata, type 00 flour or a mix of the two on my working table when handling and shaping pizza dough.

To shape Roman pizza and focaccia, make sure to have abundant flour on the counter. You want to transfer the proofed dough from the container directly onto the floured surface, let the dough fall from the proofing box onto the floured counter and dust more flour on the top. Quickly press down with your fingers starting from the top side coming down toward you to lightly dimple and flatten the dough. Flip one-third

of the dough onto your wrist and pick it up from the counter. Let gravity stretch it while you remove the excess flour from the hanging dough by gently patting it with your other hand. This is a fairly quick step. Place the stretched dough dimpled side down onto the pizza tray and pull the edges until the pizza pan is completely covered. If your dough pulls back when stretching the corners, that is a sign that your dough is underproofed. In that case, leave the dough covered in the pan and let it sit for 20 minutes. If after 20 minutes the dough still pulls back, let it sit for another 20 minutes, or until the dough easily stretches and you're able to fully cover the corners of the pan with it.

bake

We are finally ready to bake. While your dough is proofing, preheat your oven to 550°F (287°C) or as indicated in each recipe, preferably with a pizza stone set onto a rack positioned just below the fan level, and have all your ingredients ready to season your pizza or focaccia.

You want to make sure the oven is as hot as it can be to allow the pizza to bake quickly and evenly, which is why you want to set the pan onto the pizza stone. **The hot stone will quickly transfer heat to the bottom of the pan, allowing the dough to rapidly reach high temperatures.** As the dough temperature rises, carbon dioxide is released by the yeast until a temperature of 140°F (60°C) is reached where all the yeast will die off. The gas released will quickly inflate the dough, creating an airier and lighter crumb, which is why you want to bake pizza at very high temperatures.

After your pizza is stretched and shaped, season it and bake it immediately following the details indicated in each recipe.

pizza shaping step by step

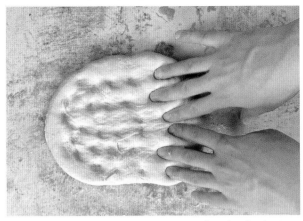

After transferring your proofed pizza dough onto a floured surface, begin pressing down with your fingertips to flatten.

Pull the bottom edge to elongate the dough.

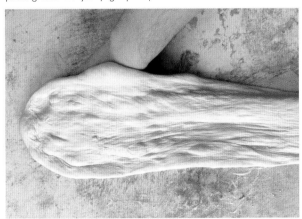

Pull and stretch the opposite edge.

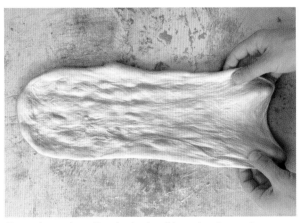

Keep pulling and stretching the dough until it matches the pan size.

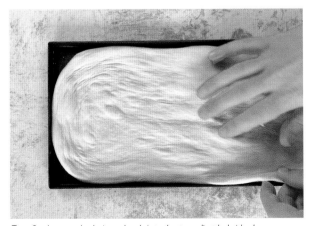

Transfer the stretched pizza dough into the pan, dimpled side down.

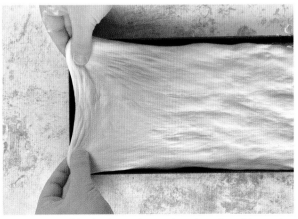

Pull the corners of the dough to make sure the entire surface of the pan is evenly covered.

focaccia shaping step by step

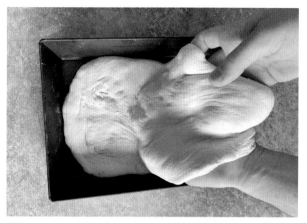

Place your proofed focaccia dough into an oiled deep pizza pan.

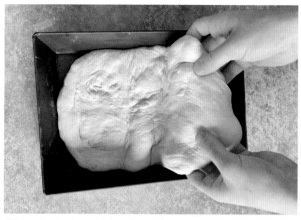

Enlarge the dough toward the edges of the pan.

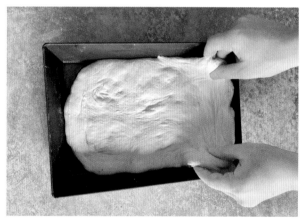

Pull the dough toward the corners of the pan.

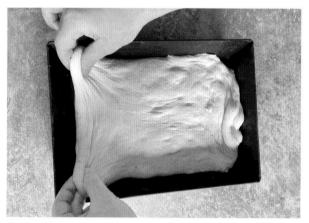

Repeat with the opposite side.

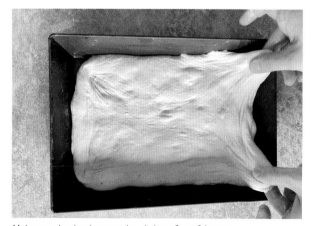

Make sure the dough covers the whole surface of the pan.

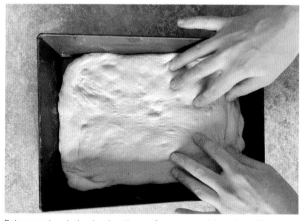

Enlarge and push the dough with your fingers toward the edges of the pan to make sure the dough is stretched evenly.

romana al taglio
quattro formaggi, wild mushroom and truffle | carbonara | potato and scamorza | broccoli and sausage

In Rome this is the "street food" pizza, the kind that is typically baked in large rectangular metal pans and sold by weight. It is called *al taglio*, meaning "cut up," because it's usually sectioned with scissors into squares. This pizza is usually handed to customers over the counter on a wooden board and enjoyed with a cold beer or wrapped up like a sandwich and consumed on the go. Today, this style of pizza has evolved into pure art. Topped with all types of elaborate gourmet seasonings, this is my favorite type of pizza and the one I bake for my friends when I host a party. Here are a few options that include some of my favorite toppings.

yield: 2 pizzas

700 g (24.69 oz) water, divided

600 g (21.16 oz) type 00 pizza flour

360 g (12.7 oz) type 0 flour

40 g (1.41 oz) type 1 flour

3 g (0.11 oz) baker's yeast

20 g (0.71 oz) salt

20 g (0.71 oz) extra virgin olive oil

Semola rimacinata, for dusting

quattro formaggi, wild mushroom and truffle

Fresh mozzarella

Smoked mozzarella

Taleggio

Gorgonzola

Wild mushrooms (chanterelles, morels, maitake, oyster mushrooms), cleaned and sliced

Grated Pecorino Romano

Grated Parmigiano Reggiano

Fresh thyme

Freshly ground black pepper

Extra virgin olive oil

Shaved fresh truffle

carbonara

Fresh mozzarella

Sliced guanciale or pancetta

Egg yolks

Grated Pecorino Romano

Freshly ground black pepper

potato and scamorza

Fresh mozzarella

Scamorza cheese or smoked mozzarella

Grated Yukon gold potatoes (2 or 3 large potatoes)

Fresh rosemary

Freshly ground black pepper

Extra virgin olive oil

Salt flakes

broccoli and sausage

3 qt (2.8 L) water

15 g (0.53 oz) salt, plus more for seasoning

1 g (0.035 oz) baking soda

2 large heads broccoli

Extra virgin olive oil

3 cloves garlic, chopped

Chili flakes

Pepper, for seasoning

2 or 3 raw sausages

Fresh mozzarella

Grated Parmigiano Reggiano

(continued)

Begin with the autolyse. In the bowl of a stand mixer fitted with the paddle attachment, add 600 grams (21.16 oz) of the water with the type 00 pizza flour, type 0 flour and type 1 flour and mix until all the water is absorbed and there are no dry bits left. This step should take no more than 2 minutes. Let the mixture sit in the mixer's bowl covered with plastic wrap in the refrigerator for 2 hours. For more details on my pizza method, see page 118.

After the autolyse, set the bowl in the stand mixer fitted with the dough hook attachment and start mixing on low (speed 3). Immediately add the baker's yeast and salt and keep mixing for 2 minutes. Increase the speed to medium-high (speed 5) and mix for 6 to 8 minutes, adding the remaining water slowly in small increments, making sure the dough absorbs it before adding more. Once all the water is fully incorporated, your dough should appear silky smooth and elastic. Reduce the speed back to low (speed 3) and slowly pour in the extra virgin olive oil, let it incorporate for a few minutes until it is fully absorbed, then turn the mixer off, transfer your dough into a proofing box covered with a lid or plastic wrap and start the bulk proof.

Let the dough sit at a temperature between 75°F and 80°F (23°C and 26°C) for 3 hours, performing one set of coil folds after 90 minutes. Place the dough covered with a lid or plastic wrap in the refrigerator for a 48-hour cold proof.

After the cold fermentation, take the dough out of the fridge and let it sit at room temperature for 30 minutes. Transfer the dough onto a lightly sprayed surface and divide it in two. Preshape the dough, giving each half a round shape by rolling it with the help of a dough scraper to form into a tight ball. Place the two preshaped doughs into separate containers covered with a lid or plastic wrap and final proof them at a temperature between 75°F and 80°F (23°C and 26°C) for 3 to 4 hours before stretching and baking.

In the meantime, preheat your oven to 550°F (287°C), setting a pizza stone on the bottom rack, and dust two 8 × 24–inch (20 × 60–cm) Roman pizza pans with the semola rimacinata.

Working with one dough at a time, transfer the dough onto a surface heavily dusted with semola rimacinata, dust more flour over the top and press down with your fingers starting from the top side coming down toward you to quickly dimple and flatten the dough. Pick up the dough and fold it over your wrist, shake off the extra flour and place it in the tray, dimpled side down. Enlarge and stretch the dough in the tray by pulling it toward the corners, making sure the dough covers the whole surface of the tray (see page 121 for step-by-step photos of this process).

For the Quattro Formaggi, Wild Mushroom and Truffle pizza, top and cover the stretched pizza with equal parts of torn up fresh mozzarella, smoked mozzarella, taleggio and gorgonzola. Lay the previously cleaned and sliced wild mushrooms on top of the cheeses and sprinkle them with grated Pecorino Romano and Parmigiano Reggiano. Finally, top with fresh thyme, freshly ground black pepper and a drizzle of extra virgin olive oil. Shave fresh truffle on top as soon as the pizza comes out of the oven.

For the Carbonara pizza, top and cover the stretched pizza with torn up fresh mozzarella and lay the thinly sliced guanciale or pancetta over the whole surface. Separate 3 or 4 egg yolks from the whites and place them into a small cup and, with a teaspoon, drizzle the broken yolks over the pizza, then sprinkle on an abundant amount of grated Pecorino Romano and finish with freshly ground black pepper.

(continued)

For the Potato and Scamorza pizza, top and cover the stretched pizza with equal parts of fresh mozzarella and scamorza cheese or smoked mozzarella. Peel the potatoes, then shred them using a box grater and place an even layer of grated potatoes on top of the cheese. Finish with picked rosemary leaves, freshly ground black pepper, extra virgin olive oil and a generous sprinkle of salt flakes.

For the Broccoli and Sausage pizza, bring the water to a boil in a medium-sized pot, then add the salt and baking soda. Adding baking soda when you blanch your greens will preserve their bright green color, as the baking soda raises the pH of the water. Cut the broccoli florets off the stem and boil them in the water until they are very soft and easy to mash. In the meantime, heat the extra virgin olive oil over medium-low heat in a medium-sized saucepan, add the garlic and chili flakes and cook for a few minutes until fragrant but not browned.

Using a fine-mesh strainer, drain the broccoli, add it to the oil and season with salt and pepper. Cook for a few minutes over medium-low heat, stirring until coarsely mashed. Set them aside to cool. Top the stretched pizza with an even layer of smashed broccoli, remove the casing from the sausages, tear them into bite-sized pieces and add them on top of the broccoli. Top the pizza with torn mozzarella cheese and sprinkle with Parmigiano Reggiano and extra chili flakes.

No matter which pizza you are making, bake it on the pizza stone in the oven at 550°F (287°C) for 10 to 15 minutes, or until golden brown, and enjoy it while it's hot.

sourdough genovese

Genovese refers to a traditional focaccia typical of the city of Genova, in the Ligurian region. This is where pesto comes from, as two of the best ingredients produced in this area are in fact basil and extra virgin olive oil, which is used abundantly on top of this focaccia. Before commercial yeast started gaining popularity among bakers about two hundred years ago, this was a product made exclusively with natural yeast. During the Roman Empire, it was made primarily with barley and rye flour, it was denser and flatbread-like and it had a longer shelf life, which made it the perfect food for travelers and fishermen. In Italy, the focaccia Genovese that is produced today uses primarily fine white flour and commercial yeast. It's a relatively quick risen dough that over time evolved into a thick focaccia that has a very soft texture with a denser crumb. To honor the long-gone tradition of this bread, I chose to make this particular recipe with sourdough starter instead of commercial yeast. The peculiarity about this focaccia is the way it's seasoned. A salamoia is drizzled over the top of the proofed dough before it enters the oven. A salamoia is nothing but an emulsion of water and extra virgin olive oil, used abundantly on focaccia Genovese to maintain a soft and fragrant top. My interpretation of Genovese is a texturally rich and flavorful product thanks to the addition of whole grain. This is also a dough that is perfectly suited as a base for different types of pizza and focaccia.

yield: 1 focaccia

350 g (12.35 oz) type 0 pizza flour

100 g (3.53 oz) type 00 flour

50 g (1.76 oz) type 1 flour

340 g (11.99 oz) water

100 g (3.53 oz) mature starter

10 g (0.35 oz) salt

10 g (0.35 oz) extra virgin olive oil

salamoia

80 g (2.82 oz) extra virgin olive oil

80 g (2.82 oz) water

to season

Salt flakes

Dried oregano

Fresh rosemary (optional)

Start by feeding your starter with equal parts water and flour 3 to 4 hours before mixing. For more details on my focaccia method, see page 118.

During the last 60 minutes of your starter fermentation, start the autolyse. In the bowl of a stand mixer fitted with the paddle attachment, combine the type 0 pizza flour, type 00 flour and type 1 flour with all of the water until the flour is fully hydrated and there are no dry bits left. This should take no more than 2 minutes. Cover the bowl with a towel or plastic wrap and let the mixture sit in the refrigerator until your starter reaches peak.

Add your mature starter to the autolysed dough and, using a stand mixer fitted with the dough hook attachment, start mixing on low (speed 2) for 3 minutes. Increase the speed to medium-high (speed 5) and keep mixing for 5 to 8 minutes. Your dough should appear silky smooth and elastic. Reduce the speed back to low (speed 2) and add the salt. Let it incorporate for 2 minutes, then slowly incorporate the extra virgin olive oil until it is fully absorbed. This will take a few minutes. Once the oil is fully incorporated, turn the mixer off, cover the bowl with a towel and let the dough rest for 15 minutes before taking it out.

Transfer your dough into a proofing box and start the bulk proof at a temperature between 75°F and 80°F (23°C and 26°C) for 3 hours, performing two sets of coil folds, once every hour.

Transfer your dough onto a lightly floured surface and preshape it by rolling it with the help of a dough scraper to form a tight ball. Place the preshaped dough into a proofing container covered with a lid or plastic wrap and place in the refrigerator for a 12-hour cold proof.

(continued)

The next day, pull the focaccia from the fridge and let it proof at room temperature for 3 hours. In the meantime, preheat your oven to 480°F (250°C), preferably setting a pizza stone on the bottom rack, and grease a 10 x 16–inch (25 x 40–cm) tray with extra virgin olive oil.

Proceed with shaping your focaccia (for step-by-step photos, see page 122). Transfer the proofed focaccia onto a floured surface, dust more flour over it and press down with your fingers starting from the top side coming down toward you to lightly dimple and flatten the dough.

Flip the enlarged dough onto your wrist and let gravity stretch it while you remove the excess flour from the hanging dough by gently patting it with your other hand. This is a fairly quick step. Place the stretched dough dimpled side down onto the pizza tray and pull the edges until the pizza pan is completely covered.

Pull the corners of the focaccia to make sure the dough covers the entire surface of the pan and let the dough rest covered at room temperature for 1 hour.

In the meantime, make your salamoia by simply combining the extra virgin olive oil with the water, preferably in a squeeze bottle or any container with a lid. Gently dimple your focaccia with oiled fingertips, vigorously shake the salamoia to emulsify it and drizzle it over the dimpled Genovese. Add a sprinkle of salt flakes and dried oregano and top with fresh rosemary, if desired.

Bake the focaccia by placing the pan onto the pizza stone at 480°F (250°C) for 15 to 20 minutes, or until golden brown.

focaccia pugliese

Pugliese refers to the style of focaccia typical of the Apulia region, the heel of Italy's "boot." When it comes to fresh food, seafood and bread, this is one of the absolute top places in Italy. Wood-fired ovens are still largely used to bake bread and focaccia across the region. Depending on the different areas, focaccia can be made with the addition of red onion, olives, potatoes or simply seasoned with sea salt and fresh rosemary. The focaccia I decided to create is a hybrid of these different types. I stretch the dough thick in a well-oiled pan so that the bottom of the dough soaks it in while baking, and I top it with a generous layer of thinly sliced raw red onions that lie in between ripened, freshly cut tomatoes. The sweet moisture of the tomatoes slowly melts the onions as the focaccia puffs up in the oven, creating a sublime and intense combination of flavors.

yield: 1 focaccia

375 g (13.23 oz) water, divided

200 g (7.05 oz) type 00 pizza flour

280 g (9.88 oz) type 0 flour

20 g (0.71 oz) semola rimacinata

2 g (0.07 oz) baker's yeast

10 g (0.35 oz) salt

20 g (0.71 oz) extra virgin olive oil

to season

1 large red onion

15–20 ripe cherry tomatoes

Fresh rosemary

Extra virgin olive oil

Dried oregano

Salt flakes

Using a stand mixer fitted with the dough hook attachment, add 280 grams (9.88 oz) of the water with the type 00 pizza flour, type 0 flour and semola rimacinata and start mixing on low (speed 2) for 2 minutes, or until all the ingredients are combined. Add the baker's yeast and salt and keep mixing for 2 minutes. Increase the speed to medium-high (speed 5) and mix for 6 to 8 minutes, adding the remaining water slowly in small increments, making sure the dough absorbs it fully before adding more. Once all of the water is fully incorporated, your dough should have gained strength and appear smooth and elastic. Reduce the speed back to low (speed 3) and slowly pour in the extra virgin olive oil. Let it incorporate for a few minutes until it is fully absorbed, then turn the mixer off and let the dough rest in the bowl for 15 minutes before taking it out. For more details on my focaccia method, see page 118.

With wet hands, pick up the dough with a circular motion, tucking it into itself to tighten lightly before placing it in a proofing box covered with a lid or plastic wrap. Let the dough sit at a temperature between 75°F and 80°F (23°C and 26°C) for 3 hours, then place it in the refrigerator for a 48-hour cold proof.

After the cold proof, take the dough out of the fridge and let it sit at a temperature between 75°F and 80°F (23°C and 26°C) for 3 hours. In the meantime, preheat your oven to 480°F (250°C), setting a pizza stone on the bottom rack, and grease a 10 × 16–inch (25 × 40–cm) pizza pan with extra virgin olive oil.

Transfer the proofed dough onto a floured surface, dust more flour over the top and press down with your fingers starting from the top side and coming down toward you to quickly dimple and flatten the dough.

Pick up the dough by folding it over your wrist, shake off the extra flour and place it in the tray, dimpled side down. Enlarge and stretch the dough in the tray by pulling it toward the corners (for step-by-step photos of this process, see page 122). Cover the tray with plastic wrap and let the dough proof for 1 more hour at room temperature. In the meantime, thinly slice the red onion, cut your cherry tomatoes in half and pick the fresh rosemary off the stem, then set them all aside.

After the last hour of fermentation, drizzle your focaccia with extra virgin olive oil, dimple it by pressing your fingertips into the dough and enlarge it if needed, making sure the dough covers all corners of the pan. Top the focaccia with the sliced onions, tomatoes, rosemary, dried oregano, salt flakes and another drizzle of extra virgin olive oil.

Bake the focaccia by placing the pan onto the pizza stone in the oven at 480°F (250°C) for 10 to 15 minutes, or until golden brown. Allow the focaccia to slightly cool in the pan for 10 to 20 minutes and enjoy it while it's warm.

whole wheat focaccia
mortadella, burrata and pistachio pesto

As you probably know by now, I am a huge fan of whole grains. The flavor and texture that this focaccia develops are incredible. Although whole grains usually make a heavier dough when used at a higher percentage, the outcome of this focaccia is still surprisingly light. This is a style of focaccia or pizza largely used in Italy and found in Roman *pizzerie al taglio* and bakeries around the city. The focaccia is typically baked plain, only seasoned with extra virgin olive oil and salt. Once baked, it is topped or filled with fresh buffalo mozzarella and cold cut meats. One of the most iconic flavor combinations in Rome is focaccia filled with thinly sliced mortadella, which we call in Roman dialect "pizza and mortazza." In this recipe, I wanted to channel those delicious squares of pizza filled with mortadella that I used to eat growing up. I elevated the rich and flavorful texture of this whole wheat focaccia with the traditional thinly sliced mortadella, creamy burrata cheese and a bright pistachio pesto. The outcome feeds the desire for indulgence, while still providing the guilt-free nutritional benefit of the whole grains.

yield: 1 focaccia

350 g (12.35 oz) water, divided

300 g (10.58 oz) type 00 pizza flour

200 g (7.05 oz) type 1 flour

2 g (0.07 oz) baker's yeast

10 g (0.35 oz) salt

10 g (0.35 oz) extra virgin olive oil

pistachio pesto

30 g (1.06 oz) fresh mint leaves

30 g (1.06 oz) fresh basil leaves

3 qt (2.8 L) water

15 g (0.53 oz) salt

1 g (0.035 oz) baking soda

70 g (2.47 oz) pistachios

150 g (5.29 oz) extra virgin olive oil

20 g (0.71 oz) lemon juice

5 g (0.18 oz) salt

1 g (0.035 oz) ground black pepper

1 clove garlic

25 g (0.88 oz) grated Pecorino Romano

25 g (0.88 oz) grated Parmigiano Reggiano

to season

Extra virgin olive oil

Dried oregano

Salt flakes

Fresh burrata

Sliced mortadella

Pistachio pesto

Fresh basil leaves

Using a stand mixer fitted with the dough hook attachment, add 280 grams (9.88 oz) of the water with the type 00 pizza flour and type 1 flour and start mixing on low (speed 2) for 2 minutes, or until all the ingredients are combined. Add the baker's yeast and salt and keep mixing for 2 minutes. Increase the speed to medium-high (speed 5) and mix for 6 to 8 minutes, adding the remaining water slowly in small increments, making sure the dough absorbs it fully before adding more. Once all the water is fully incorporated, your dough should have gained strength and appear smooth and elastic. Reduce the speed back to low (speed 3) and slowly pour in the extra virgin olive oil. Let it incorporate for a few minutes until it is fully absorbed, then turn the mixer off and let the dough rest in the bowl for 15 minutes before taking it out. For more details on my focaccia method, see page 118.

With wet hands, pick up the dough with a circular motion, tucking it into itself to tighten lightly before placing it in a proofing box covered with a lid or plastic wrap. Let the dough sit at a temperature between 75°F and 80°F (23°C and 26°C) for 3 hours, then place it in the refrigerator for a 48-hour cold proof.

After the cold proof, take the dough out of the fridge and let it sit at a temperature between 75°F and 80°F (23°C and 26°C) for 3 hours.

(continued)

In the meantime, preheat your oven to 480°F (250°C), setting a pizza stone on the bottom rack, and grease a 10 x 16–inch (25 x 40–cm) pizza pan with extra virgin olive oil.

Proceed with making the pistachio pesto. Pick the mint and basil leaves off the stems and set them aside. Bring the water to a boil in a medium-sized pot. Add the salt and baking soda. Adding baking soda when you blanch your greens will preserve the bright green color as the baking soda raises the pH of the water. Set up your blanching station. Have a bowl filled with ice water next to the pot of boiling water and lay a kitchen towel next to the bowl.

Working in batches, place the basil and mint leaves in a medium-sized strainer and blanch them in the boiling water for 5 seconds, stirring the leaves quickly in the water for even blanching. Rapidly transfer the strainer into the ice bath for a few seconds, or until the leaves are cold, then place the basil and mint onto the towel. Dipping the strainer in the boiling water will help you contain the leaves, allowing you to quickly remove them from the water and transfer them into the ice bath to cool. Once all the leaves are blanched, tightly roll them into the towel and twist it over a kitchen sink to squeeze out the excess water. Using a food processor, blend the blanched mint and basil with the pistachios, extra virgin olive oil, lemon juice, salt, ground black pepper, garlic, grated Pecorino Romano and grated Parmigiano Reggiano. Transfer the pesto into a container and set it aside. The leftover pesto can be stored in the refrigerator for up to 7 days or frozen for future use.

Transfer the proofed dough onto a floured surface, dust more flour over the top and press down with your fingers starting from the top side, working down toward you to quickly dimple and flatten the dough. Pick up the dough by folding it over your wrist, shake off the extra flour and place it in the tray dimpled side down. Enlarge and stretch the dough in the tray by pulling it toward the corners (for step-by-step photos of this process, see page 122). Cover the tray with plastic wrap and let the dough proof for 1 more hour at room temperature.

After the last hour of fermentation, drizzle your focaccia with extra virgin olive oil, dimple it by pressing your fingertips into the dough and enlarge it if needed, making sure the dough covers all corners of the pan. Season with dried oregano and salt flakes and drizzle with more extra virgin olive oil. Bake the focaccia on the pizza stone in the oven at 480°F (250°C) for 10 to 15 minutes, or until golden brown.

Transfer the focaccia onto a wire rack and allow it to slightly cool for 15 to 20 minutes, then top it with burrata, mortadella, a spoonful of pistachio pesto and finish it with fresh basil leaves. Enjoy it while it is warm.

focaccia al tegamino

figs and duck prosciutto

Just like Pizza Rossa (page 141) and Whole Wheat Focaccia—Mortadella, Burrata and Pistachio Pesto (page 132), this is another recipe that takes me back to my younger years spent in Rome. The pizza and fig combination has a history spanning more than two thousand years. In fact, during the Roman Empire, a bread resembling a mix between a focaccia and a flatbread called "schiacciata di pane" was widely available from bakeries around Rome. It was the bread mostly consumed by peasants and the lower class. They would pick figs off the trees that surrounded the city and top the bread with them to make it more substantial and nutritious. Over time, almost two millennia later, this bread has evolved into a soft and airy focaccia filled with ripened figs and sometimes with the addition of thinly sliced prosciutto. This is one of Rome's iconic late summer snacks when figs are at their peak.

In this recipe, I wanted to highlight the tradition of "pizza and figs" while baking the figs on the focaccia dough so that the fruit will caramelize for extra sweetness. I have also topped it with sliced fresh figs for a pop of brightness and duck prosciutto for a gamey salty contrast. Duck prosciutto is a specialty item and I strongly recommend you try it. It is likely not available at your local grocery store, but it is widely accessible online. If you prefer, it is also perfectly suitable to substitute with a more readily available prosciutto.

yield: 2 focaccia

370 g (13.05 oz) water, divided

300 g (10.58 oz) type 00 pizza flour

200 g (7.05 oz) type 0 flour

2 g (0.07 oz) baker's yeast

10 g (0.35 oz) salt

25 g (0.88 oz) extra virgin olive oil

to season

Extra virgin olive oil

Fresh figs

Salt flakes

Duck prosciutto

Using a stand mixer fitted with the dough hook attachment, add 280 grams (9.88 oz) of the water with the type 00 pizza flour and type 0 flour and start mixing on low (speed 2) for 2 minutes, or until all the ingredients are combined. Add the baker's yeast and salt and keep mixing for 2 minutes. Increase the speed to medium-high (speed 5) and mix for 6 to 8 minutes, adding the remaining water slowly in small increments, making sure the dough absorbs it fully before adding more. Once all the water is fully incorporated, your dough should have gained strength and appear smooth and elastic. Reduce the speed back to low (speed 3) and slowly pour in the extra virgin olive oil. Let it incorporate for a few minutes until it is fully absorbed, then turn the mixer off and let the dough rest in the bowl for 10 minutes before taking it out. For more details on my focaccia method, see page 118.

With wet hands, pick up the dough from the bowl with a circular motion, tucking it into itself to tighten lightly before placing it in a proofing box covered with a lid or plastic wrap. Let the dough sit at a temperature between 75°F and 80°F (23°C and 26°C) for 2 hours, then place the dough covered with a lid or plastic wrap in the refrigerator for a 48-hour cold proof.

After the cold fermentation, take the dough out of the fridge and let it sit at room temperature for 30 minutes. Transfer the dough onto a lightly sprayed surface and divide it in two. Preshape it by giving each half a round shape, rolling with the help of a dough scraper to form into a tight ball. Place the two preshaped doughs into separate containers covered with a lid or plastic wrap and final proof them at a temperature between 75°F and 80°F (23°C and 26°C) for 3 hours.

In the meantime, preheat your oven to 480°F (250°C), setting a pizza stone on the bottom rack, and grease a 10-inch (25-cm) round cast-iron skillet with extra virgin olive oil.

(continued)

Working with one dough at a time, transfer the proofed dough onto a floured surface, dust more flour over the top and press down with your fingers starting from the top side working down toward you to quickly dimple and flatten the dough.

Pick up the dough by folding it over your wrist, shake off the extra flour and place it in the skillet dimpled side down. Enlarge and stretch the dough in the pan by pulling it toward the edges and cover it with plastic wrap. Let the dough proof for 1 more hour at room temperature and in the meantime place the other dough in the refrigerator until you're done baking the first focaccia.

After the last hour of fermentation, drizzle extra virgin olive oil onto the proofed focaccia and dimple by pressing your fingertips into the dough. Quarter 5 or 6 figs and gently press the segments into the dough dimples. Sprinkle the focaccia with salt flakes and place the cast-iron pan onto the pizza stone in the oven. Bake it at 480°F (250°C) for 20 to 25 minutes, or until golden brown.

Transfer the focaccia onto a wire rack and allow it to slightly cool for 10 to 20 minutes, then top it with sliced fresh figs and thinly sliced duck prosciutto. Enjoy it while it's warm.

margherita napoletana

The origin of pizza as we know it is from Naples. It is believed that the first pizza was made for Queen Margherita in the late 1800s. A chef was asked to create a treat for her and what he baked was a dough stretched and seasoned with tomatoes, mozzarella and fresh basil. These ingredients were widely available in the area around Naples. After baking his creation in a wood-burning oven, he named it after the queen. There it was, the first pizza Margherita. The white dough, red sauce and green basil also mirrored the colors of the Italian flag. Neapolitans are particularly proud and protective of the legacy of their traditions. Pizza now takes many forms and variations around the globe, but in Naples the authentic pizza Napoletana has to have specific characteristics. A legitimate Margherita Napoletana has a thick crust called "cornicione" and a thin center that holds up a sauce made with tomatoes from the area, usually San Marzano, as well as fresh mozzarella. Before entering the oven, it's finished with extra virgin olive oil, and after it's baked it is topped with fresh basil leaves. Margherita Napoletana's beauty is in its simplicity. A baker cannot hide behind any bells and whistles when baking a Margherita. It is simply judged on the technique and lightness of the dough, the flavor of the sauce and the quality of the cheese.

yield: 6 pizzas

620 g (21.87 oz) water, divided

300 g (10.58 oz) type 00 pizza flour

700 g (24.69 oz) type 0 flour

2 g (0.07 oz) baker's yeast

20 g (0.71 oz) salt

to season

Tomato Sauce (page 116)

Fresh mozzarella

Extra virgin olive oil

Fresh basil leaves

Using a stand mixer fitted with the dough hook attachment, add 550 grams (19.4 oz) of the water with the type 00 pizza flour and type 0 flour and start mixing on low (speed 2) for 2 minutes, or until all the ingredients are combined. Add the baker's yeast and salt and keep mixing for 2 minutes. Increase the speed to medium-high (speed 5) and mix for 8 to 10 minutes, adding the remaining water slowly in small increments, making sure the dough absorbs it fully before adding more. Once all the water is fully incorporated, your dough should have gained strength and appear white and smooth. Turn the mixer off and let the dough rest in the mixer for 10 minutes before taking it out. For more details on my pizza method, see page 118.

With wet hands, pick up the dough from the bowl with a circular motion, tucking it into itself to tighten lightly before placing it in a proofing box covered with a lid or plastic wrap. Let the dough sit at a temperature between 75°F and 80°F (23°C and 26°C) for 3 hours. Have a 3-inch (8-cm)-deep pizza proofing box ready and transfer the dough onto a nonfloured surface, divide it into six and preshape it by giving each segment a round shape, rolling with your hands or with the help of a dough scraper to form each into a tight smooth ball.

Place the six preshaped pizzas into the proofing box evenly distanced from each other, cover it with a lid or plastic wrap and place it in the refrigerator for a 48-hour cold proof.

After the cold fermentation, take the dough out of the fridge and let it sit at a temperature between 75°F and 80°F (23°C and 26°C) for 3 to 4 hours before baking.

In the meantime, preheat your oven to 550°F (287°C), setting a pizza stone on the bottom rack.

(continued)

Have your tomato sauce, mozzarella and fresh basil ready and proceed with shaping your pizza. Generously flour your countertop and, working with one dough at a time, transfer one preshaped pizza onto the floured surface by scooping up the round dough with a dough scraper. Dust more flour on the top. Begin pressing down with your fingertips starting from the center and moving outward, pushing the air trapped in the dough to the edges. This will create the typical thick and airy crust. Keep pressing the center of the dough with your fingers and enlarge it by rotating and stretching it outward as you press it, making sure to keep the center thinner than the edges.

Clear the excess flour from underneath the dough and season it with a large spoonful of sauce in the center. With the back of the spoon spread the sauce in a circular motion up to the edge, leaving at least 1 inch (2.5 cm) of it clear of sauce.

Top the pizza with torn-up fresh mozzarella and a drizzle of extra virgin olive oil and slide it onto a pizza peel. Once on the peel, simultaneously pull the opposite edges of the shaped pizza with your hands to enlarge the dough so it fully covers the peel. Slide the pizza onto the preheated pizza stone and bake it for 5 to 8 minutes, or until the crust browns evenly. Top with fresh basil leaves once out of the oven.

pizza rossa

This recipe holds a special place for me in this book because it's the pizza I took to school for lunch almost every day growing up. This style is called "*pizza alla pala*" because it's stretched onto a long wooden peel or "*pala*" and baked in deck ovens. Originally this was made using leftover bread dough that was stretched thin and baked with simple seasonings like tomato sauce or potatoes. Although this pizza shares the same city of origin, it differs from the Romana al Taglio (page 123) due to the way the pizza is baked. Locals are known to refer to this specialty as "*Lingua Romana*," which means "Roman tongue," due to the shape of the final product, which is an oblong disc with a very thin crust. This dough incorporates semola rimacinata to add a rustic and hearty texture. In this recipe, I wanted to re-create my favorite basic variation of *pizza rossa* meaning "red pizza," because the star here is the sauce. I love the simplicity of this recipe because it allows the quality of the ingredients to shine through.

yield: 2 pizzas

500 g (17.64 oz) water, divided

150 g (5.29 oz) type 00 pizza flour

525 g (18.52 oz) type 0 flour

75 g (2.65 oz) semola rimacinata

2 g (0.07 oz) baker's yeast

15 g (0.53 oz) salt

20 g (0.71 oz) extra virgin olive oil

to season

Tomato Sauce (page 116)

Extra virgin olive oil

Begin with the autolyse. In the bowl of a stand mixer fitted with the paddle attachment, add 400 grams (14.11 oz) of the water with the type 00 pizza flour, type 0 flour and semola rimacinata and mix until all the water is absorbed and there are no dry bits left. This should take no more than 2 minutes. Let the mixture sit in the bowl covered with plastic wrap in the refrigerator for 2 hours. For more details on my pizza method, see page 118.

After the autolyse, set the bowl in the stand mixer fitted with a dough hook attachment and start mixing on low (speed 3). Immediately add the baker's yeast and salt and keep mixing for 2 minutes. Increase the speed to medium-high (speed 5) and mix for 8 to 10 minutes, adding the remaining water slowly in small increments, making sure the dough absorbs it fully before adding more. Once all the water is fully incorporated, your dough should have gained strength and appear smooth and elastic. Reduce the speed back to low (speed 3) and slowly pour in the extra virgin olive oil. Let it incorporate for a few minutes until it is fully absorbed, then turn the mixer off, transfer your dough into a proofing box covered with a lid or plastic wrap and start the bulk proof.

Let the dough sit at a temperature between 75°F and 80°F (23°C and 26°C) for 3 hours, performing one set of coil folds after 90 minutes. Place the dough covered with a lid or plastic wrap in the refrigerator for a 48-hour cold proof.

After the cold fermentation, take the dough out of the fridge and let it sit at room temperature for 30 minutes. Transfer the dough onto a lightly sprayed surface and divide it in two. Preshape your dough, giving each half a round shape by rolling with the help of a dough scraper to form it into a tight ball. Place the two preshaped doughs into separate containers covered with a lid or plastic wrap and final proof them at a temperature between 75°F and 80°F (23°C and 26°C) for 3 to 4 hours before stretching and baking.

In the meantime, preheat your oven to 550°F (287°C), setting a pizza stone on the bottom rack, and dust two 8 x 24–inch (20 x 60–cm) Roman pizza pans with semola rimacinata.

(continued)

Working with one dough at a time, transfer it onto a surface heavily dusted with semola rimacinata, dust more flour over the top and press down with your fingers starting from the top side and working down toward you to quickly dimple and flatten the dough.

Pick up the dough by folding it over your wrist, shake off the extra flour and place it in the tray dimpled side down. Enlarge and stretch the dough in the tray by pulling it toward the corners, making sure the dough covers the whole surface of the tray (for step-by-step photos of this process, see page 121).

Season the pizza with a thin layer of tomato sauce, drizzle extra virgin olive oil on top and place the pan onto the pizza stone in the oven. Bake it at 550°F (287°C) for 10 to 15 minutes, or until the crust is dark golden brown.

Slide the pizza onto a wire rack and let it cool slightly. Top it with fresh extra virgin olive oil and enjoy it while it's warm.

sfilatini
olives and sun-dried tomatoes

These sfilatini are a quick and easy way to impress guests by making a snack to be enjoyed as an aperitivo with a cheese board and your favorite vino. This recipe is also a delicious way to avoid waste by giving you an option on how to utilize leftover dough, which can come from any of the recipes in this chapter. If you haven't just made pizza, you can start from scratch with the recipe below. Although this recipe uses traditional flavors like sun-dried tomatoes, olives and oregano, you can feel free to be playful and try your own combinations. You may also divide this dough in two and shape half of it like sfilatini and the other half can be proofed and baked into a delicious focaccia of its own, maybe topped with fresh rosemary and extra virgin olive oil.

yield: 20–22 sfilatini

640 g (22.58 oz) water, divided

400 g (14.11 oz) type 00 flour

160 g (5.64 oz) semola rimacinata

440 g (15.52 oz) type 0 flour

3 g (0.11 oz) baker's yeast

20 g (0.71 oz) salt

200 g (7.05 oz) sun-dried tomatoes in olive oil

200 g (7.05 oz) sliced Kalamata olives

to season

Extra virgin olive oil

Dried oregano

Salt flakes

Using a stand mixer fitted with the dough hook attachment, add 540 grams (19.05 oz) of the water with the type 00 flour, semola rimacinata and type 0 flour and start mixing on low (speed 2) for 2 minutes, or until all the ingredients are combined. Add the baker's yeast and salt and keep mixing for 2 minutes. Increase the speed to medium-high (speed 5) and mix for 6 to 8 minutes, adding the remaining water slowly in small increments, making sure the dough absorbs it fully before adding more. Once all the water is incorporated, the dough should have gained strength and appear smooth and elastic. Turn the mixer off and let the dough rest in the bowl for 20 minutes.

With wet hands, pick up the dough from the bowl with a circular motion, then transfer it into a proofing box and add all the sun-dried tomatoes and olives. Give the dough a quick set of coil folds and begin the bulk proof. For more details on my pizza and focaccia method, see page 118.

Cover the proofing box with a lid or plastic wrap and let the dough sit at a temperature between 75°F and 80°F (23°C and 26°C) for 3 hours, performing three sets of coil folds, once every hour, to strengthen the dough and evenly distribute the olives and sun-dried tomatoes. Place the dough in the refrigerator for a 12-hour cold proof.

After the cold fermentation, take the dough out of the fridge and let it sit at a temperature between 75°F and 80°F (23°C and 26°C) for 3 hours. In the meantime, preheat your oven to 480°F (250°C), setting a pizza stone on the bottom rack.

Dust a large Roman pizza pan or a half sheet pan with semola rimacinata and then proceed with shaping your sfilatini. Working on a surface with abundant semola rimacinata, cut your dough into 100-gram (3.53-oz) pieces and gently roll each one into an elongated shape measuring approximately 30 inches (76 cm) long. Take one end of the thin roll and bring it to meet the other one to create two strips of dough of the same length. Pinch the two ends together and start twisting by rolling with both hands, moving in opposite directions to evenly twist the dough.

Place your shaped sfilatini twists onto the sheet pan and brush them with extra virgin olive oil. Sprinkle dried oregano and salt flakes on top and bake them at 480°F (250°C), setting the pan onto the pizza stone, for 10 to 15 minutes, or until golden brown. Enjoy them warm.

Pastry

I have a very strong passion for sweets. Growing up in Italy, the art of pastry making was on display everywhere. Just like with bread, wine, cheese and pasta, pastries have a long history and vary across the different regions in Italy. My whole family would gather for Sunday lunch at my grandma's. The meals were always followed by large trays of pastries and sweets from the local bakery, plus the cookies and tarts my grandmother would bake from scratch. I would follow her closely and help pick fresh fruits and nuts from her garden that we would use to make these amazing desserts. When I think of sweets, I immediately associate the word with joy and playfulness. I believe pastries are meant to be shared, and in this chapter I take some of the food memories from my childhood, like Croissants (page 149) and bomboloni (page 162), and elevate them with all I have learned through my years as a trained chef. My goal is to show you the tips and tricks that will elevate your pastry skills and allow you to bake delicious treats to enjoy with your friends and family.

croissants

My passion for croissants dates back to my childhood. A freshly baked warm croissant and a foamy cappuccino were my breakfast every day in Rome. My obsession with making croissants, however, began a few years ago when I tried laminating my first batch at home. From that moment I realized what I was up against. This is hands down one of the most intricate and challenging techniques to master, and I instantly became obsessed with perfecting my croissants. I started testing ingredient ratios and different flours until I finally baked a croissant that was perfectly flakey and buttery. When I finally settled on this formula, I was absolutely ecstatic with the results. I have developed a dough that is relatively easy to work with, perfect for hand lamination, but rivals the quality of the best baked croissants of a bakery. Make sure you plan ahead when starting to make croissants, as the whole process is a two-day endeavor. With this recipe, I want to equip you with all the details and the exact directions on how I go about making croissants with the hope that you embark on a journey toward perfecting your own.

yield: 12–15 croissants

lamination

500 g (17.64 oz) butter sheet

croissant dough

260 g (9.17 oz) water

260 g (9.17 oz) whole milk

20 g (0.71 oz) baker's yeast

450 g (15.87 oz) high-protein wheat flour

450 g (15.87 oz) all-purpose flour

120 g (4.23 oz) sugar

15 g (0.53 oz) salt

40 g (1.41 oz) unsalted butter

egg wash

1 whole egg

1 egg yolk

15 g (0.53 oz) whole milk

butter and lamination

To make croissants, you have to consider two key components: the main dough (called *détrempe*) and the butter sheet for lamination.

Lamination is the process that combines the butter sheet into the dough by performing sets of rolling and folding the two together in order to form alternating layers. The goal when laminating is to keep the butter and the dough cold at all times. This allows the dough to be stretched thin, with the butter functioning as a "divider" between layers, which results in the light and open honeycomb structure typical of a croissant.

Butter plays a fundamental role in developing the characteristic flavor of a croissant. I strongly suggest sourcing a butter sheet specifically designed for laminated doughs. They are sold in 2.2-pound (1-kg)-thin, rectangular shapes and widely available online. My go-to brand is the French Isigny Ste Mére. I find it extremely important to source the best ingredients, and they are undoubtedly one of the top brands around.

The reason why it is important to use a butter designed for laminated dough is not only the fact that it's shaped and ready to be incorporated into the dough but also because it's a butter with less moisture. It contains a higher percentage of butterfat than regular store-bought brands (usually above 83%), which gives it a higher melting point, making this type of butter **more stable when exposed to warm temperatures**.

However, if you wish to use a different product to laminate your croissants, I suggest sourcing a good-quality, organic European-style butter and shaping the sheet yourself. Leave the 500 grams (17.64 oz) of butter at room temperature to soften for a few hours or overnight and place it in between two sheets of parchment paper. With the help of a flexible dough scraper, flatten and smooth the butter into a 10 × 7–inch (25 × 18–cm) rectangle approximately ½ inch (1.3 cm) thick (see page 151 for step-by-step photos of this process). I suggest you shape your butter sheet 1 or 2 days in advance and reserve it in the refrigerator until it is needed.

(continued)

A key factor to consider when handling your butter sheet is temperature. If the butter is too warm, the sheet will be too soft and it will melt into the dough as you roll it. The result? Your baked croissant crumb will be dense and most likely end up looking like a brioche. If the butter is too cold and the sheet is a solid block of butter, it will be very challenging to roll it and it will tend to easily break as you apply pressure. In this case, the butter won't distribute evenly throughout the dough, creating an uneven crumb.

The butter sheet should be pliable, soft enough that you can bend it without breaking it, but hard enough that when you hold it, it won't melt in your hands. As mentioned earlier, temperature is the only way you can control the texture of your butter sheet. Depending on the temperature of your environment, you may want to place the butter sheet in and out of the freezer for a few minutes as needed, trying to maintain an ideal temperature between 55°F and 60°F (12°C and 15°C) when combining it with the dough.

mix and proof your dough

Proceed with mixing your croissant dough the evening before you plan on making croissants. You want to mix and proof the dough overnight—for 12 hours—so that you allow the cold fermentation to build flavor. Also, it's crucial that your dough is cold when you laminate, which will facilitate the layering of the butter during this step.

Using a stand mixer fitted with the dough hook attachment, mix the water, whole milk, baker's yeast, high-protein wheat flour, all-purpose flour, sugar, salt and unsalted butter together on low (speed 1) for 3 minutes, then increase the speed to medium-low (speed 3) and mix for 12 minutes. Turn the mixer off, cover the bowl with a towel and let the dough rest in the bowl for 10 minutes before taking it out. The mixing time for this type of dough is relatively short, and the reason for that is because you don't want to develop too strong of a gluten structure, as the dough will keep strengthening when laminating. I found that for this recipe 15 minutes is enough to evenly combine the ingredients and create the perfect structure that will facilitate lamination.

Transfer the dough onto a nonfloured surface and give it a round shape, using both hands to roll and tuck the dough two or three times until it is formed into a homogeneous ball.

Roll the dough loosely in two sheets of parchment paper, making sure the dough is completely wrapped to protect it from drying out and to control moisture while proofing. Then place it in a plastic container. The dough will double in size, so choose a proofing box that is big enough, seal it tightly with a lid or plastic wrap and place it in the refrigerator at 39°F (4°C) for 12 hours.

Pull your butter sheet from the fridge the evening before laminating and leave it at room temperature overnight to soften.

(continued)

butter sheet

Place your softened butter between two parchment paper sheets.

Begin rolling toward the corners with a rolling pin to flatten the butter.

Continue rolling to evenly enlarge and form your butter sheet.

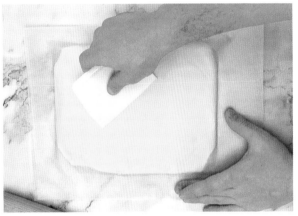

With the help of a dough scraper, flatten the butter to approximately ½ inch (1.3 cm).

Push the dough scraper against the parchment along the edges to mold the butter sheet into a rectangular shape.

Make sure to keep molding the butter sheet using the dough scraper until evenly flat.

laminate your dough

Roll the dough into a 10 x 14–inch (25 x 35–cm) rectangle, about ½ inch (1.3 cm) thick.

Place the butter sheet in the middle.

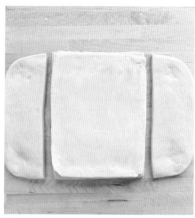

Cut the two edges with a sharp knife or a pizza roll.

Place the cut dough on top of the butter.

Make sure the two doughs meet in the center, covering the whole butter surface evenly.

Start pressing down and rolling the dough with a rolling pin.

Fold one-third of the rolled dough over the center.

Fold the opposite third of the dough over the center.

The dough should overlap evenly with the edges perfectly aligned.

Cut along the folded edge with a sharp paring knife.

Repeat on the opposite folded edge.

Proceed with rolling the dough.

Fold one-third of the rolled dough over the center.

Fold the opposite third over itself to meet the other edge.

Fold the dough in half one last time.

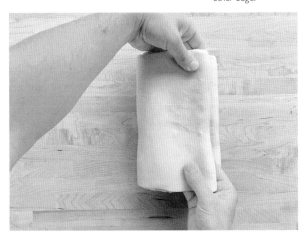

Make sure the two halves are evenly folded.

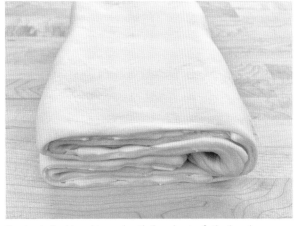

The dough should overlap evenly with the edges perfectly aligned.

laminate your dough

Pull the proofed dough from the fridge and place it onto a lightly floured surface. Using a rolling pin, roll the dough into a 10 x 14–inch (25 x 35–cm) rectangle of approximately ½-inch (1.3-cm) thickness.

Place the butter sheet in the middle of the rolled dough, cut the two flaps of excess dough left on each side and place them on top of the butter, making sure they meet in the center and cover all corners. The dough should encase the butter completely.

Lightly flour the top and bottom of the dough. Using a rolling pin, press down to flatten then roll to a ¾-inch (2-cm) thickness and make a single fold. Bring one-third of the dough from the left side over to the center and fold one-third of the dough on the right side over the left one, creating three layers of dough.

Place the folded dough onto a sheet tray lined with parchment paper, cover it with plastic wrap and place it in the refrigerator for 40 minutes. This rest period will help your dough cool down and will relax the gluten structure, making it easier to repeat more sets of folds.

Proceed with performing the second fold, this time a double fold. Using a sharp paring knife, cut along the two folded edges to facilitate even rolling. Lightly flour the top and bottom of the dough and press down again with your rolling pin to flatten it. Roll it to ¾ inch (2 cm) thick and fold the left side to three-quarters over the opposite side, fold the right side over to meet the folded left side of the dough, then fold the longer folded side over again to create a four-layer dough this time. Place the laminated dough onto a sheet tray lined with parchment paper, cover it with plastic wrap and place it in the refrigerator for another 40 minutes. (See images on pages 152 to 153 for step-by-step photos of this process.)

shape and bake your croissants

Now it's time to roll the dough one final time and shape your croissants. Again, using a sharp paring knife, cut along the three folded edges to facilitate even rolling and roll the dough to ¼ to ⅓ inches (6 to 8 mm) thick. Using a chef's knife or a pizza cutter, trim a thin layer off the edges to even out the rectangle and cut your croissants into approximately 4 x 10–inch (10 x 25–cm) triangles (see page 155 for step-by-step photos).

Shape the croissants by lightly stretching the triangle by pulling the tip then rolling it tightly, starting from the base of the triangle. After they have been shaped, your croissants are ready to be proofed and baked or they can be frozen for future use. If you decide to freeze your croissants, always store them in an airtight container in between parchment paper layers and make sure you defrost them in the refrigerator overnight before proofing and baking for a better and more consistent result. However, your croissants could also be proofed directly from frozen. Note that the length of proofing time will almost double if you use this method. You may want to proof them this way overnight to bake them first thing in the morning and enjoy them with fresh coffee.

Proof your croissants on a sheet tray lined with a baking mat or parchment paper at a temperature between 70°F and 73°F (21°C and 23°C) for 3 to 4 hours. Cover the tray with plastic wrap, making sure the plastic doesn't come into contact with the croissants to prevent sticking.

Preheat your oven to 400°F (200°C). Once the croissants are almost done proofing, make the egg wash by whisking the whole egg, egg yolk and whole milk together in a bowl. Gently brush the tops of your croissants with the egg wash right before baking, and as soon as you put the croissants in the oven, drop the temperature to 350°F (175°C). Bake them for 15 to 20 minutes, or until golden brown.

shaping your croissants

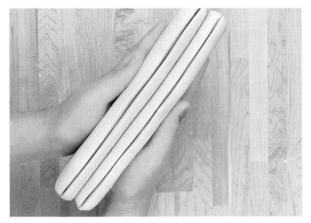

Cut along the folded edges with a sharp paring knife on both sides.

Press down and roll the dough with a rolling pin.

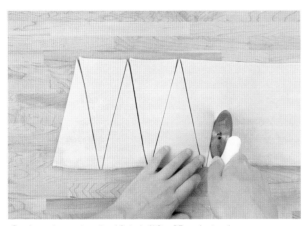

Cut the croissants into 4 x 10–inch (10 x 25–cm) triangles.

Gently stretch to elongate the triangle before rolling the croissant.

Roll the laminated dough tightly to form the croissant.

Finish rolling with the seam on the bottom.

black raspberry and chamomile rolls

Among the many shapes and forms that a croissant dough can take, there is one I particularly love, and that is a Danish. The classic Danish that I used to eat in Rome growing up is a rolled laminated dough filled with chocolate chips, typically topped with vanilla custard piped in the center of the roll just before entering the oven. This recipe is an upgraded Danish, a hybrid version between a Danish and a roll. I wanted to highlight the layers of a perfectly laminated dough by twisting it before rolling each one into a coil. The contrast between a chunky black raspberry jam and a velvety custard makes this roll bright and rich. A floral and soothing chamomile glaze smoothly covers the roll, keeping all the flavors in balance. I love foraging for my own berries and making preserves when I can. I have tried many versions of this recipe, with flavors and inclusions ranging from apricot, peach, chocolate and hazelnut to pistachio rose and white chocolate, just to name a few. I hope this extremely versatile technique will stimulate your creativity and satisfy your appetite for new and delicious flavor combinations.

yield: 10–12 rolls

1 batch Croissant dough (page 149)

chamomile glaze

200 g (7.05 oz) whole milk

10 g (0.35 oz) dried chamomile flowers

5 g (0.18 oz) lemon juice

300 g (10.58 oz) powdered sugar

black raspberry custard

1 lemon

500 g (17.64 oz) whole milk

6 egg yolks

140 g (4.94 oz) sugar

1 fresh vanilla bean, scraped

45 g (1.59 oz) pastry flour, sifted

100 g (3.53 oz) black raspberry jam

egg wash

1 whole egg

1 egg yolk

15 g (0.53 oz) whole milk

Follow the recipe for Croissant dough on page 149. While mixing the main dough the night before, begin making your chamomile glaze. Warm the whole milk slightly and combine it with the dried chamomile flowers. Immediately pour the soaked flowers and the milk into an airtight plastic bag or a container covered with a lid and let them steep overnight in the refrigerator.

The next day, drain the milk through a fine-mesh strainer. It should yield 140 grams (4.94 oz) of chamomile-infused milk. Reserve it in the refrigerator for later use.

Begin making the black raspberry custard. Peel half of the lemon and, in a small saucepan, add the milk and lemon peel and bring them to a gentle boil over medium heat. In a second small saucepan, add the egg yolks, sugar, the scraped vanilla bean and the sifted pastry flour. Whisk them to combine for 30 seconds, or until the mixture is smooth. Set it aside.

Once the milk comes to a boil, turn the heat off and ladle one-third of it into the pan with the egg yolk mixture and quickly whisk them to combine for a few seconds until all the ingredients form a homogeneous liquid. Add the rest of the milk to the mix, discarding the lemon peel, and set the pan over medium-low heat. Stir continuously using a whisk to prevent scorching until the custard comes to a boil. Keep simmering the custard for 2 minutes, then remove it from the heat and pour it into a bowl or a small sheet tray. Set a layer of plastic wrap against the custard, making sure to cover the whole surface to prevent it from drying out, and place it in the refrigerator to cool.

Once it is completely cold, transfer the custard into a mixing bowl and fold the black raspberry jam into it. Store it in the refrigerator.

Roll your croissant dough to ¼ to ⅓ inches (6 to 8 mm) thick and, using a chef's knife or a pizza cutter, trim a thin layer off the edges to even out the rectangle.

Spread a layer of custard onto half of the dough and fold the other half over it. Cut the dough into 1-inch (2.5-cm) strips. Twist each strip into a spiral and roll it into a circular shape (for step-by-step photos, see page 158).

(continued)

Preheat your oven to 400°F (200°C). Proof your rolls on a sheet tray lined with a baking mat or parchment paper at a temperature between 70°F and 75°F (21°C and 24°C) for 2½ to 3 hours. Cover the tray with plastic wrap, making sure the plastic doesn't come into contact with the croissants to prevent sticking.

Make the egg wash by whisking the whole egg, egg yolk and whole milk together in a bowl, then gently brush the tops of the rolls with it. As soon as you put the rolls in the oven, drop the temperature to 350°F (175°C) and bake them for 15 to 20 minutes, or until golden brown.

While your rolls cool, prepare your chamomile glaze. In a medium-sized mixing bowl, combine the chamomile-infused milk with the lemon juice and powdered sugar. Whisk them until they are smooth and pour the glaze over the rolls to coat them completely.

Spread an even layer of the black raspberry custard onto half of the laminated dough.

Fold the opposite half of the dough over the custard.

Cut the dough into 1-inch (2.5-cm) strips.

Twist each strip to capture the custard in between the two dough halves.

Start rolling one side of the twist into a coil.

The coil should be rolled tight and look as round as possible.

chocolate cherry sourdough bread pudding

Chocolate and cherry are a classic combination that I particularly enjoy in all types of baked goods. The chocolate flavor comes from the dark cocoa powder and the addition of roughly chopped dark chocolate that melts into tiny pockets when this loaf is baked. The dried cherries are presoaked in Grand Marnier to further compound the fruit flavor with orange and add notes of rich oak and vanilla. I wanted to include this sourdough in the pastry section because of its decadence. This is a loaf that can be enjoyed by itself, but it really shines when repurposed. In fact, I have included details on how to transform this bread into a decadent and rich bread pudding. The sourdough loaf is submerged in a Grand Mariner crème anglaise. Pecans and more cherries are folded in right before baking to create a compound of flavors that will surely impress your guests.

yield: 2 loaves

chocolate cherry sourdough

150 g (5.29 oz) dried tart cherries

350 g (12.35 oz) Grand Marnier

400 g (14.11 oz) high-protein wheat flour

170 g (6 oz) all-purpose flour

25 g (0.88 oz) dark cocoa powder

490 g (17.28 oz) water

150 g (5.29 oz) mature starter

15 g (0.53 oz) salt

120 g (4.23 oz) 70% dark chocolate

crème anglaise

450 g (15.87 oz) whole milk

250 g (8.82 oz) heavy cream

60 g (2.12 oz) Grand Marnier

6 egg yolks

150 g (5.29 oz) sugar

Zest of 1 large orange

1 fresh vanilla bean

for the pudding

Crème anglaise

1 chocolate cherry loaf

250 g (8.82 oz) dried tart cherries

300 g (10.58 oz) Grand Marnier

150 g (5.29 oz) chopped pecans

Powdered sugar, for dusting

Begin by soaking the dried tart cherries in Grand Marnier and let them sit overnight at room temperature.

The next day, feed your starter with equal parts water and flour 3 to 4 hours before mixing.

During the last 60 minutes of your starter's fermentation, start the autolyse. In the bowl of a stand mixer fitted with the paddle attachment, combine the high-protein wheat flour, all-purpose flour and dark cocoa powder with the water until the flour is fully hydrated and there are no dry bits left. This should take no more than 2 minutes. Cover the bowl with a towel or plastic wrap and let the mixture sit at room temperature until your starter reaches peak.

Add your mature starter to the autolysed dough and, using a stand mixer fitted with the dough hook attachment, mix on low (speed 2) for 3 minutes. Increase the speed to medium-high (speed 5) and keep mixing for 5 to 8 minutes, or until the dough has gained strength and is smooth and elastic. Reduce the speed back to low (speed 2) and add the salt. Let it incorporate for 2 minutes, then turn the mixer off, cover the bowl with a towel and let the dough rest for 15 minutes in the bowl before taking it out.

Transfer your dough into a proofing box and start the bulk proof at a temperature between 75°F and 80°F (23°C and 26°C) for 4 hours, performing three sets of coil folds, once every hour.

Drain and add the cherries to the dough when performing the first coil fold and the dark chocolate with the second fold. Don't worry if it looks like the chocolate and cherries are not evenly absorbed right away at the first set of folds. They will distribute evenly throughout the bulk fermentation as you keep performing folds.

Transfer your dough onto a lightly floured surface, divide it in two and preshape it by giving each half a round shape, rolling with the help of a dough scraper to tighten the ball. Cover it with a towel and let it rest for 1 hour at room temperature or in a proofing chamber.

Proceed with shaping the batards (page 29).

(continued)

chocolate cherry sourdough
bread pudding (continued)

Dust two 10-inch (25-cm) oval bannetons with flour and transfer each loaf into the basket, seam side up, then cover them with a towel and place them in the refrigerator for a final cold proof at 39°F (3.9°C) for 12 to 16 hours.

Preheat your Dutch oven to 500°F (260°C), line it with a piece of parchment paper and place the loaf in the Dutch oven. Bake the loaf with the lid on at 500°F (260°C) for 10 minutes, drop the temperature to 450°F (232°C) and keep baking with the lid on for 10 minutes. Take the lid off, drop the temperature to 430°F (215°C) and finish baking for 15 to 20 minutes, or until dark brown.

Remove the bread from the oven, place it on a wire rack and allow it to cool for at least 30 minutes to 1 hour before slicing into it.

You can now enjoy your chocolate sourdough as is, or take it a step further and turn this delicious loaf into a bread pudding. The decision is yours!

Begin making the crème anglaise. Fill one-quarter of a medium saucepan with water and simmer it over medium-low heat. Combine the whole milk and heavy cream with the Grand Marnier in a separate medium-sized saucepan and bring it to a simmer over medium-low heat.

In a medium-sized mixing bowl, add the egg yolks, sugar and orange zest. Cut the vanilla bean in half lengthwise and with a paring knife, scrape out the seeds, add them to the bowl and whisk until all the ingredients are combined.

As soon as the milk comes to a simmer, remove the pan from the heat. Scoop up a full ladle of the simmering liquid and add it to the egg mixture. Quickly whisk them together until homogeneous and set the mixing bowl over the simmering saucepan with water.

Pour the rest of the liquid into the bowl and constantly stir the mixture with a whisk or a rubber spatula. Using a digital thermometer, monitor the temperature of the mixture as you keep stirring and remove the bowl from the heat when the crème anglaise reaches 180°F (82°C).

Pour the crème anglaise into a heatproof container, cover it with plastic wrap and place it in the refrigerator until it is completely cool.

Cut one whole chocolate cherry loaf into 2-inch (5-cm) cubes and place them into a mixing bowl. Pour the cooled crème anglaise over the cubes and press them down with a spatula, making sure the bread starts absorbing the liquid. Lay a sheet of plastic wrap over the bowl, making sure it is in contact with the mixture, then press down with your hands to make sure the bread is completely submerged in the crème anglaise. Place the bowl in the refrigerator and let the bread soak overnight.

Place the dried cherries in a plastic container and pour the Grand Mariner over them. Cover the container with a lid and let them soak overnight.

The next day, preheat your oven to 340°F (170°C). Drain the cherries and fold them into the soaked bread followed by the chopped pecans. Transfer the mixture into a buttered 10-inch (25-cm) round cast-iron pan and bake it for 45 minutes to 1 hour, or until dark golden brown.

Let the pudding cool slightly, dust it with powdered sugar and enjoy it warm.

espresso and milk chocolate sourdough bomboloni

Bomboloni is the Italian word for "donuts." It was one of my favorite cravings coming back home from a late night out. This bomboloni recipe is a favorite for coffee and chocolate lovers alike. The rich and velvety milk chocolate custard filling is decadent with an equally powerful coffee punch. I developed this filling based on an inspiration from a coffee and chocolate ganache tart I used to make as a young cook. The dough is made lighter and softer by the addition of steamed potatoes and the orange zest gives mild citrus notes, making this dough deliciously versatile. For example, after being deep fried to a golden brown, it can be glazed with different flavors or simply tossed in cinnamon sugar.

yield: 12–18 bomboloni

espresso custard

550 g (19.4 oz) whole milk

150 g (5.29 oz) whole coffee beans

100 g (3.53 oz) egg yolks

80 g (2.82 oz) sugar

1 fresh vanilla bean

60 g (2.12 oz) pastry flour, sifted

170 g (6 oz) milk chocolate

bomboloni

75 g (2.65 oz) Yukon gold potatoes

50 g (1.76 oz) unsalted butter

200 g (7.05 oz) mature starter

200 g (7.05 oz) whole milk

120 g (4.23 oz) whole eggs (2 large)

25 g (0.88 oz) sugar

500 g (17.64 oz) high-protein wheat flour

Zest of 1 orange

10 g (0.35 oz) salt

to fry

Vegetable oil

Sugar, for tossing

Begin by making the espresso custard. Slightly warm the whole milk. Place the whole coffee beans into an airtight plastic bag or a container, then pour the warm milk over them and place them in the refrigerator to soak overnight.

The next morning, feed your starter with equal parts water and flour 3 to 4 hours before mixing and proceed with making the custard.

In a small saucepan, add the egg yolks, sugar, the scraped vanilla bean and the sifted pastry flour. Whisk them to combine for 30 seconds, or until the mixture is smooth. Set it aside.

Line a medium strainer over a small saucepan and filter the coffee-soaked milk. Discard the beans and bring the milk to a gentle boil over medium heat.

Once boiling, turn the heat off and ladle one-third of the milk into the pan with the egg yolk mixture and quickly whisk them to combine for a few seconds until all the ingredients form a homogeneous liquid.

Add the rest of the milk to the mix and set the pan over medium-low heat. Stir continuously using a whisk to prevent scorching until the custard comes to a boil. Keep simmering the custard for 2 minutes, then remove it from the heat, add the milk chocolate to the hot custard and whisk vigorously to incorporate.

Pour the custard into a bowl or a small sheet tray, set a layer of plastic wrap against the top, making sure to cover the whole surface of the custard to prevent drying out and place it in the refrigerator to cool. Once completely cold, transfer the custard into a pastry bag and store it in the refrigerator.

Prepare your steamed potatoes. Place a steamer basket or a colander in a large pot. Add water until it reaches 1 or 2 inches (2.5 or 5 cm) below the bottom of the basket. Put the potatoes in the basket and bring the water to a boil. Once the water is boiling, cover the pot, reduce the heat to medium and allow the potatoes to steam until you can insert a paring knife without resistance, 30 minutes. Using tongs, remove the potatoes from the steamer basket and let them rest for 5 minutes. Peel them while they're hot, cover them loosely with plastic wrap and place them in the refrigerator to cool completely.

(continued)

Soften the unsalted butter at room temperature for at least 2 hours, or pull it from the fridge the night before.

Proceed with making the bomboloni. In a stand mixer fitted with the dough hook attachment, mix the mature starter, whole milk, whole eggs, sugar, high-protein wheat flour and orange zest for 3 minutes on low (speed 2). Increase the speed to medium-high (speed 5) and mix for 8 to 10 minutes, or until the dough has formed a strong gluten structure and is smooth and elastic.

Lower the speed back to low (speed 2) and add the salt. Let it incorporate for 2 minutes, then add the softened butter and keep mixing until it is fully incorporated. This will take a few minutes. Monitor the temperature of your dough with a digital thermometer. It should not exceed 78°F (26°C). Once the butter is fully incorporated, let the dough rest in the mixer for 10 minutes before taking it out.

Pick up the dough, give it a smooth round shape by folding it a couple of times into itself and place it into a proofing box or a bowl. Bulk proof the dough for 6 hours at a temperature between 75°F and 80°F (24°C and 26°C) as indicated in the Master Sourdough Method (page 22).

Perform four sets of coil folds, once every hour for the first 4 hours of the bulk proof, then let the dough rise for the final 2 hours.

Transfer the dough onto a lightly floured large sheet tray and roll it to a ½-inch (1.3-cm) thickness. Cover the tray with plastic wrap and let it proof at room temperature for 3 hours before cutting and frying.

Place the tray with the rolled dough in the refrigerator for the last 30 minutes of the final rise to facilitate cutting and transferring the bomboloni from the tray into the hot oil.

While the dough rises, preheat 3 inches (7.5 cm) of vegetable oil in a cast-iron pan or a large saucepan to 360°F to 370°F (182°C to 187°C).

Line a wire rack or a few layers of paper towel onto a sheet tray and set it next to the frying pan.

Pour sugar into a large bowl that you will utilize for tossing the bomboloni after frying.

Using a 3-inch (7.5-cm) ring cutter, cut your bomboloni and fry them in batches of three or four at a time in the hot oil for 2 minutes per side, or until golden brown.

Transfer the fried bomboloni to the wire rack for a few seconds to drain the excess oil before tossing them in the sugar.

Let your bomboloni cool slightly before filling them with the espresso custard. Enjoy them while they're still warm.

triple chocolate babka

When I made my first chocolate babka a few years ago, I was hooked. I love how versatile this recipe is. You can fill it with anything, and since then I've been experimenting with so many sweet and savory combinations. The secret to perfectly thin and defined layers when rolling babka is to work with cold dough. The amount of fat in the dough helps the mass to harden when cool, facilitating rolling and cutting, which helps in braiding a perfect babka. In this case I wanted to create a version that is absolutely rich and decadent, filled with a fudgy chocolate spread with, the addition of chocolate chips that melt into liquid pockets when baked and covered entirely with a dark chocolate glaze.

yield: 1 loaf

brioche dough

65 g (2.29 oz) unsalted butter

220 g (7.76 oz) whole milk

1 large egg

2 g (0.07 oz) vanilla extract

50 g (1.76 oz) sugar

445 g (15.7 oz) high-protein wheat flour

Zest of 1 large orange

12 g (0.42 oz) baker's yeast

10 g (0.35 oz) salt

chocolate filling

110 g (3.88 oz) 70% dark chocolate

80 g (2.82 oz) unsalted butter

90 g (3.17 oz) dark brown sugar

30 g (1.06 oz) cocoa powder

140 g (4.94 oz) dark chocolate chips

chocolate glaze

180 g (6.35 oz) 70% dark chocolate

90 g (3.17 oz) unsalted butter

Begin by softening the unsalted butter at room temperature for at least 2 hours, or pull it from the fridge the night before.

Using a stand mixer fitted with the dough hook attachment, mix the whole milk, egg, vanilla extract, sugar, high-protein wheat flour, orange zest, baker's yeast and salt on low (speed 2) for 3 minutes. Increase the speed to medium-high (speed 5) and keep mixing for 8 to 10 minutes, or until the dough has gained strength and is smooth and elastic. Reduce the speed back to low (speed 3), add the softened butter and let it incorporate until it is fully absorbed. This will take a few minutes. Monitor the temperature of your brioche with a digital thermometer. It should not exceed 78°F (26°C). Once the butter is fully incorporated, let the dough rest in the mixer for 10 minutes before taking it out.

Pick up the dough, give it a smooth round shape by folding it a couple of times into itself and place it in a bowl. Proof the dough for 60 to 90 minutes at a temperature between 75°F and 80°F (24°C and 26°C). The dough should double in size.

Transfer your brioche dough to a lightly floured surface and with the help of a rolling pin roll it into a ¼-inch (6-mm)-thick rectangle. Transfer the dough onto a sheet tray lined with parchment paper. Cover it with plastic wrap and place it in the refrigerator for 1 hour.

While your brioche cools down, begin making the chocolate filling by melting the dark chocolate and butter in a bowl placed over a small saucepan simmering with 2 inches (5 cm) of water or in the microwave. Once the chocolate and butter are melted, remove the bowl from the heat and whisk in the brown sugar and cocoa powder for a few seconds, or until incorporated, then set it aside to cool.

Butter a 13-inch (33-cm) pullman loaf pan.

Pull your brioche dough from the fridge, transfer it onto a lightly floured countertop, trim ½ inch (1.3 cm) of dough off the edges and with the help of an offset spatula spread the chocolate filling evenly over the rectangle up to the edges. Sprinkle the chocolate chips over the filling and starting with the long side roll the dough into a tight coil.

(continued)

triple chocolate babka (continued)

With a sharp knife, cut and split the rolled dough in half lengthwise to expose the filling, cross the two halves to form the letter X and twist them together as if you were braiding them (for step-by-step photos on shaping a babka, see page 97). Place the shaped babka into the buttered loaf pan and proof it for 1 hour at a temperature between 75°F and 80°F (24°C and 26°C).

Preheat your oven to 360°F (182°C). Bake your babka for 15 to 20 minutes, or until golden brown. Place it on a rack and let it cool.

Save the trimmed edges and reshape them into small buns or roll them into fritters and proof them with your babka. Then either bake them with the babka or deep fry them at 350°F (176°C) in vegetable oil.

Make the glaze by melting the chocolate and butter in a bowl sitting over a small saucepan simmering with 2 inches (5 cm) of water or in the microwave. Set it aside and once the babka is completely cool, pour it over the top. Let the glaze cool for a couple of hours until hard and set before cutting into your babka.

honey lavender cream puffs

These cream puffs are the ultimate crowd pleaser. Lavender-infused cream is whipped with mascarpone and vanilla for an extra rich mousse. The addition of honey complements the floral notes of lavender, creating a delicate and not overly sweet filling. I incorporated a technique to make craquelin, which is simply a mixture of butter, sugar and flour rolled into a thin layer and cut in a perfect circle. Pâte à choux is baked to perfection and topped with the buttery disc just before entering the oven. The craquelin will melt before your eyes as the puffs rise, quickly setting over the surface to create a crunchy and luxurious layer. You are sure to impress your guests with these stunning and delicious cream puffs.

yield: 20–25 cream puffs

mascarpone mousse

10 g (0.35 oz) lavender flowers

280 g (9.88 oz) heavy cream

350 g (12.35 oz) mascarpone

150 g (5.29 oz) honey

1 fresh vanilla bean

Zest of 1 lemon

craquelin

100 g (3.53 oz) unsalted butter, softened

100 g (3.53 oz) sugar

60 g (2.12 oz) pastry flour

40 g (1.41 oz) almond flour

pâte à choux

140 g (4.94 oz) whole milk

140 g (4.94 oz) water

125 g (4.41 oz) unsalted butter

2 g (0.07 oz) salt

185 g (6.53 oz) bread flour

260 g (9.17 oz) whole eggs (4 large)

to garnish

Bee pollen (optional)

Powdered sugar

To make the mascarpone mousse, begin by placing the lavender flowers into a heatproof container. Slightly warm the heavy cream in a saucepan and pour the liquid over the dried flowers. Cover it with a lid and place it in the refrigerator to infuse overnight.

The next day, start by making the craquelin. Using a food processor or a stand mixer fitted with the whisk attachment, combine the softened unsalted butter, sugar, pastry flour and almond flour for 2 to 3 minutes, or until smooth.

Line a large parchment paper sheet or a silicone mat and use a flexible dough scraper to transfer the mixture onto the middle of the paper and lay another sheet on top. With the help of a rolling pin, roll the mixture to a ⅛-inch (3-mm) thickness and refrigerate it.

Proceed with making the pâte à choux. Combine the whole milk, water, unsalted butter and salt in a heavy saucepan and bring it to a gentle simmer over medium heat. Remove the pan from the stove and, away from the heat, add all the bread flour at once, stirring quickly until it is completely absorbed.

Return the pan to the stove over medium heat and stir vigorously until the mixture forms a homogeneous ball and pulls away from the sides of the pan. This step will take no more than 2 minutes.

Transfer the mixture to the bowl of a stand mixer fitted with the paddle attachment. If you wish to do this step by hand, leave the dough in the pan. Start mixing on low (speed 3), using a digital thermometer to monitor the temperature of the dough. Keep mixing until it cools down to 140°F (60°C). It should still be warm, but not too hot to the touch.

Increase the speed to 8 and start adding the eggs one at a time, waiting until each egg is completely absorbed before adding the next. When all the eggs are incorporated, the paste is ready to use.

Preheat your oven to 340°F (170°C). Cut off the very tip (less than ½ inch [1.3 cm]) of a pastry bag to create a pocket for the air to escape. That way, when you press the pâte à choux into the bag, there's a place for the air to escape and you'll be able to fill the bag with no air pockets in the mixture. Place a round metal tip in the bag and down to the tip. Fold the bag at least halfway down over your hand, ensuring the top edge is clear and folded all the way down so you can keep it clean. Use the side of your hand to scrape the mixture off the spatula and fill the bag with the pâte à choux.

(continued)

honey lavender cream puffs (continued)

Pipe your puffs into 2-inch (5-cm)-diameter rounds on a sheet tray lined with parchment paper or a silicone baking mat.

Pull the cold craquelin from the fridge and using a 2-inch (5-cm) ring, cut as needed. Place each disc on top of the piped pâte à choux and bake it for 25 minutes, or until golden. Remove it from the oven and set it aside to cool completely.

While your puffs cool down, proceed with finishing the mascarpone mousse. Pull the lavender-infused cream from the fridge and filter the liquid over a fine-mesh strainer into a stand mixer bowl. Add the mascarpone, honey, scraped vanilla bean and lemon zest. With the whisk attachment, start whipping the mousse on speed 7 for 1 minute, or until smooth and homogeneous.

Fill a pastry bag with the mousse following the steps listed above for the pâte à choux, but this time use a star piping tip. Cut the baked puffs in half and using a 1½-inch (4-cm) ring cut the top half of the craquelin to smooth the edges. Fill the bottom half with the mousse and sprinkle bee pollen (if using) over it. Place the craquelin half on top and dust it with powdered sugar.

You may pipe any leftover pâte à choux onto a tray lined with parchment paper and freeze the puffs for future use. After the puffs are frozen, they can be stored in an airtight container in the freezer for up to a month. This same dough can also be used to make éclairs. Note that you may bake the puffs or éclairs directly from frozen or let them defrost in the refrigerator prior to baking.

acknowledgments

To my beautiful mother, Patrizia Fontana: I wouldn't be the man I am today without the many sacrifices you have made and challenges you have overcome to raise me. I deeply admire your resilience and kindness. Thank you for loving and supporting me unconditionally every step of the way and for always believing in me and encouraging me to pursue what I love.

To my little brother, Gianluca Brenci: Even though you're a grown man now, you will always be my little brother. I'm so proud of the man you have become. I miss skipping school to snuggle on the couch and watch hours of cartoons before we'd start wrestling until one of us would get seriously hurt. Thanks for always being there for me. I love you.

To my friends: I am extremely grateful for all of those I call friends today, the ones I have met throughout my journey and those who were there since I was only a little boy. If I am the man, chef and baker I am today, it is thanks to the many people who have touched my life deeply and inspired me in many ways, professionally and not.

To Anthony Ambelitos, aka the Bread Boss: You are a great friend and the most talented and knowledgeable baker I know and my go-to guy when I have any bread-related questions. Thank you for always having an answer for me, for sharing your grains and being a great inspiration and for always being available. Your support really pushes me to do better.

To my followers and supporters: I can't begin to describe how thankful I am for each and every one of you. Thank you from the bottom of my heart for being part of my journey and appreciating my work. You encourage me every day to do better and push myself. This book wouldn't have been possible without your support, and I dedicate it to all of you.

Finally, to Page Street Publishing: Thanks to Emily and Sarah and everyone on the team who has worked on putting this book together. You guys have done a tremendous job guiding me through the process and making this such a fun project to be a part of.

about the author

Chef Daniele Brenci quickly fell in love with the artistry of cooking at a young age. He grew up in Rome, a culinary Mecca that shaped the way he perceives food. He was also influenced by the quality time he got to spend with his grandmother in her kitchen and garden. Daniele takes immense pride in his Italian heritage, which built the foundation for his profound passion for food. At the age of 15, he decided to officially pursue becoming a chef and began training in different restaurants and 5-star hotels in Rome while attending culinary school. His eagerness to take opportunities when they presented themselves led him to venture all over the globe learning about different cultures, new cuisines and dynamic flavor combinations. After spending 12 years training and working in Michelin-starred restaurants and hotels in Rome, London, Malibu and Chicago, he decided to explore the private chef world. This work started with different households in Malibu and Hollywood and finally led to Pittsburgh, Pennsylvania. In the past few years he has dedicated himself to self-education on the art of baking and studying the different varieties of grains, a knowledge base he enthusiastically shares with others. He began documenting his baking journey through his Instagram @_breadcumb, where he was able to share his passion across a wider platform and become part of an inspiring community of professionals and passionate at-home cooks.

index